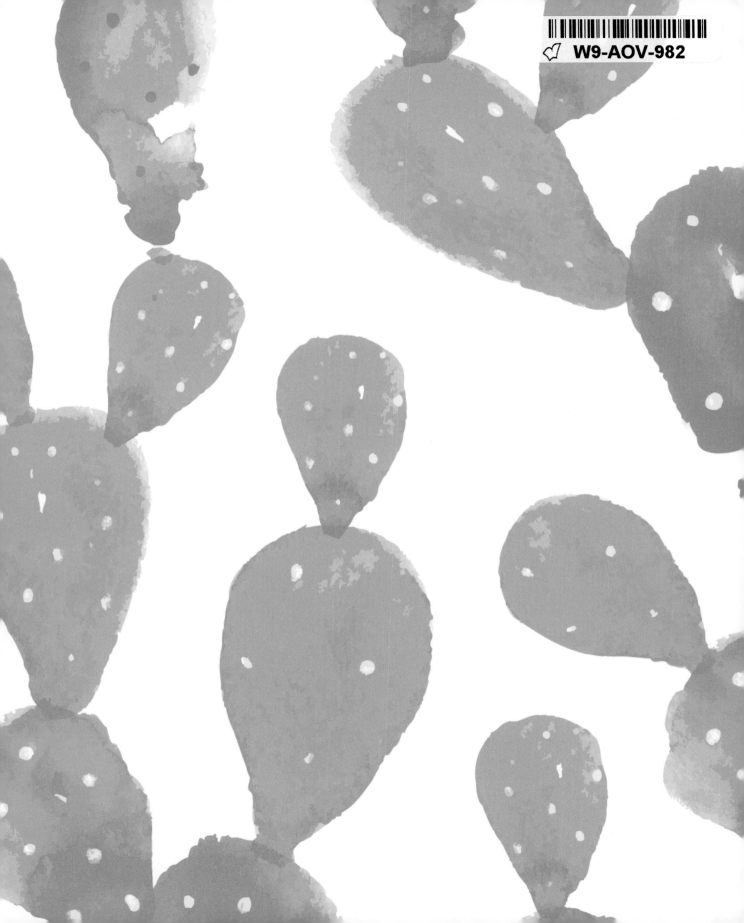

¡BUEN PROVECHO!

Traditional Mexican Flavors from My Cocina to Yours

ERICKA SANCHEZ

Published by Familius LLC, www.familius.com
PO Box 1249, Reedley, CA 93654

Familius books are available at special discounts for bulk purchases,
whether for sales promotions or for family or corporate use.
For more information, contact Familius Sales at orders@familius.com.

Library of Congress Control Number: 2021937149

Print ISBN 978-1-64170-565-3
Ebook ISBN 978-1-64170-618-6
KF 978-1-64170-590-5
FE 978-1-64170-604-9

Printed in China

Edited by Ashlin Awerkamp and Spencer Skeen
Cover design by Carlos Guerrero and Mara Harris
Book design by Mara Harris

10 9 8 7 6 5 4 3 2 1

First Edition

To my husband, Efrain, for your constant love and support,
and to my mother, Carmen, for instilling your love of cooking in me.

CONTENTS

My Mexican Kitchen

Tortillas

Salsas

Breakfast — Desayuno

Appetizers — Botanas

Salads – Ensaladas

Soups and Stews – Sopas y Guisos

Sides – Guarniciones

Mains – Platos Fuertes

Drinks — Bebidas

Desserts — Postres

Holidays — Dias Festivos

My Mexican Kitchen

INTRODUCTION

I consider myself very lucky to have grown up in a humble home where there was always a warm home-cooked meal. My mother taught me how to prepare many traditional Mexican dishes at an early age. Therefore, my boredom cure was cleaning pinto beans of *piedritas y basuritas* (pebbles and debris) and learning how to identify the correct side of the tortilla where the filling goes. (Yes! There is a correct side!)

I was born in Torreón, a city in the state of Coahuila, Mexico. Torreón is also part of *la comarca lagunera* (the lagoon region); it's a medium-sized city about 160 miles from the state capital, Saltillo. Torreón was known for manufacturing cotton but eventually transformed into a center of iron and steel mills and a petrochemical plant.

My father, mother, brother, sister, and I lived in a small house in a busy neighborhood lined with a mix of homes turned into businesses; my uncle's accounting office was a few doors down the street, and every other house had some sort of business set up at their door. I had a *raspados* shop, a *tortilleria*, and a candy store a few steps away from my house. Neighbors came and went. Everyone shared the food they were most proud of with each other, and no one ever went hungry. It was a wonderful, caring community.

My father, a traveling salesman, sold small kitchen appliances and pharmaceuticals. For many years it was just my mother, brother, sister, and me at home. My mother cooked for us three meals a day. For our school lunch, my mom walked to the elementary school daily with my younger sister in a stroller and delivered scrambled egg and chorizo tortas with a small thermos of *café con leche* to us. Yes, we drank heavily sweetened milky coffee as young kids. Those were the days, right?

By the time I was eight years old, we made the move to El Paso, Texas. My father, with broken English, found a job as a car salesman. We rented a house and made it a home. It took some time to furnish the home. I remember eating standing up to a counter or fighting with my brother over a suitcase to use as a seat. We didn't have furniture, but we always had a home-cooked meal.

With zero words of English in my vocabulary, I started third grade. No more torta deliveries from my mom—we got a free school lunch! I clearly remember being given a purple ticket and not knowing what it was for. One of my classmates told me it's "*para tu lonche.*" Lonche? In Spanish, a *lonche* is a sandwich or torta; the word for "lunch" is *almuerzo*. I was confused but just followed everyone to the cafeteria, which I had no idea existed in schools. Turns out *lonche* is just Spanglish for "lunch." Getting free school lunch was a pleasant surprise.

My first school cafeteria meal in the United States was enchiladas. I was expecting something similar to the enchiladas my mom prepared for us at home. They weren't. The enchilada sauce was mild but salty, and they were filled with cheddar cheese. That was the first time I ever experienced cheddar cheese, and it was glorious!

After our move to El Paso, I continued to visit my grandmother in Torreón at her small grocery store called *Miscelánea Dulce*, named after my cousin. I spent every summer with her until her passing in 1989, and I am very grateful I had that time with her. She taught me how to run a business, treat customers with respect, and, most importantly, feel comfortable in the kitchen. I looked forward to her impromptu cooking lessons every day. As soon as I heard her shuffling around the kitchen, I'd rush over and see what we would be preparing. I miss her dearly.

As time passed, my family grew accustomed to life in the United States. We eventually learned English and continued our education. When we kids got home from school, my mom was always there, waiting for us with a warm bowl of *sopa fideo* or a stack of freshly made tortillas. Whenever we wanted fast food, she'd say, "*Hay frijoles en la casa.*" ("There are beans at home.") She says that to this day, and I use that line on my son all the time now.

Now why *¡Buen Provecho!*? *Buen provecho* is a polite way to say "enjoy your meal" and be cordial with people. It has many meanings: *provecho* means "benefit" or "advantage," so *buen provecho* could also mean "I hope this meal benefits you well." "*Buen provecho*" is heard often at restaurants and is something you say to your loved ones. In return, you will get a "*gracias, igualmente*" or a big mouthful smile of appreciation.

This book represents my appreciation for and the deep meaning of the home-cooked meal. If there is a home-cooked meal, there is love. The recipes in this book are presented the way I was taught to make them. Many are traditional and may be very familiar to you. Others I have created or modernized myself with ingredients available to me in California, where I live now. I hope you enjoy cooking these foods as much as I enjoy sharing my recipes with you.

ESSENTIAL TOOLS

Mexican cooks take great pride in the tools they use to create a meal. Many of those treasured tools have been passed down from generation to generation. Others are meaningful wedding gifts or travel purchases. Here are my most treasured kitchen tools I use on a regular basis.

TAMALERA: A large pot used to steam tamales or other foods. The original tamalera was made of clay. Now, tamaleras are made of different materials. The pot is constructed with a rack at the bottom to prevent the tamales from getting wet. When tamales steam in the tamalera, they are usually covered by corn husks or a kitchen towel to prevent any steam from escaping, even though the pot is covered with a lid.

MOLCAJETE Y TEJOLOTE: The Mexican version of mortar and pestle, made out of stone or clay and used to grind various ingredients. The molcajete (mortar, or bowl) has three short legs. Most traditionally, the molcajete is used to crush fresh or roasted fruits and vegetables to make salsas, sauces, and marinades.

MOLINILLO: A wooden whisk used to foam Mexican hot chocolate. The molinillo design is complex and beautiful. It is carved in one piece with multiple rotating rings and a sphere at the tip. When preparing Mexican chocolate, the molinillo handle is placed between the palms and rolled back and forth quickly to aerate the liquid and create froth.

TORTILLERA: Tortilla warmer basket made out of palm leaves or plastic used to keep tortillas warm at the dinner table. The cloth tortillera is a round bag with a large opening to insert warm tortillas; it resembles a large pocket.

COMAL: A metal or cast-iron disc used to cook tortillas, roast vegetables and dried chiles, and toast nuts and seeds for sauces. Originally made of fragile unglazed clay, the comal evolved into a durable tool that could be transported and heated over firewood, on the grill, over coals, and on any gas stove burner.

MACHACADOR DE FRIJOLES: Similar to a potato masher, this utensil is a flat metal disc with holes attached to a wood or plastic handle. This tool is essential to mash whole cooked beans, such as when making refried beans, to give them texture during the frying process.

CAZUELA DE BARRO: A wide, short glazed clay pot used to cook stews, soups, and moles. When such recipes call for a cooking pot, you can use a cazuela. Most are conical-shaped to retain heat and cook evenly. Cazuelas can be big enough to feed hundreds of people, or small enough to serve as a decorative salsa container on the dinner table.

PRENSADOR DE TORTILLAS: Tortilla press. Made out of metal or wood, this contraption is a crucial tool to flatten corn masa in order to prepare perfectly round and uniform tortillas. To use the press, place a masa ball in the center, close the press, and apply pressure. This will flatten the masa ball into a tortilla shape.

TYPES OF CHILES
Dried Chiles

A few of the sauce, stew, and enchilada recipes in this book call for dried chiles. Dried chiles can be found at any Mexican or Latin American market in the produce or spice section. If they are not available in a store, they can be found online.

When shopping for dried chiles, make sure their skin has a bright sheen, with the exception of dried chipotle. Fresher dried chiles are flexible and shouldn't break apart when bent.

Store dried chiles in a dry, dark area of your pantry in an airtight container. Use within six months of purchase or they will lose their heat and flavor.

CASCABEL: The cascabel chile is a round dried chile that rattles when shaken, hence the name *cascabel* (rattle). In fresh form, it is known as chile bola. Moderately spicy, its flavor is pleasant and slightly nutty. Chile cascabel is normally prepared as a sauce with spicier chiles and red or green tomatoes. Like other dried red chiles, cascabel can be made into salsa and added to potato or meat stews.

PUYA: Similar in color and flavor to chile guajillo, chile puya is smaller and thinner (about 3 to 4 inches long). Its heat is drier and more intense than guajillo, but it's coveted for its pleasant pungent flavor, fruity undertones, and aroma. When ground up as chile flakes, it's perfect for salsas, sauces, and seasoning.

OAXACA: Oaxaca is the perfect chile for mole sauce and bean dishes. It's smoke-dried and significantly hotter than traditional pasilla chiles but milder than dried chipotle chiles. Its heat is sharp and flavorful but not overwhelming.

PASILLA NEGRO: Also known as *chile Morelia*, pasilla negro is a dark and spicier variety of chile ancho. It's very aromatic with sweet undertones. This chile is used in mole and enchilada sauces and is perfect for stews and adobos. It can also be stuffed with a mild filling.

ANCHO: Wide (*ancho*) and heart-shaped, ancho is the dried version of poblano chile and is widely used in traditional Mexican recipes. Its flavor is sweet, smoky, and bold but mild in heat. It's great for enchilada sauces, rubs, and marinades. Chile ancho is readily available in most supermarkets.

CHIPOTLE: Chipotle means "smoked pepper" in Nahuatl (*chilpoctli*). The name can be misleading because any smoked chile can be referred to as chipotle. Most commonly, though, chipotle refers to jalapeños. The dried chiles' color varies depending on the stage the fresh jalapeños were dried at. Green jalapeños take on the lighter tan chipotle color, while smoked red jalapeños are a deeper brick color. Their spicy and smoky flavor is perfect as *adobados* or an addition to *escabeche*. If large enough, chipotle chiles can be stuffed with a mild filling.

GUAJILLO: A versatile dried chile used in many Mexican dishes, guajillo is also referred to by many other names, such as *chilaca*, *cualchero*, and *travieso*. In fresh form, it is called chile mirasol. Chile guajillo is added to stews, sauces, and pozoles mainly for its bright red color. Because its flavor is very mild and fruity, it is usually used with other dried red chiles to intensify flavor and heat.

PEQUIN: Also known as *piquín*, these chiles are small, but their heat is mighty. They make sauces or stews hotter with their nutty, citrusy, and smoky flavor, or they can be crushed into a powder to add a spicy kick to your food.

Fresh Chiles

Fresh chiles can be a wonderful flavor booster to your meals. If you prefer your dish to be less spicy, carefully remove the veins and seeds with a paring knife or small spoon. It's a good idea to wear gloves during this process to keep your hands from burning. If you happen to experience "hot chile hands," remove the capsaicin (chile residue) from your hands with rubbing alcohol or dissolve it with a bit of vegetable or olive oil.

MANZANO: With its apple-like shape, yellowish-orange to red color, and citrus undertones, this friendly-looking chile isn't what you expect. The manzano is twice as hot as the jalapeño, which makes it an excellent chile for salsa and hot sauces. Because its skin is very thick, it's perfect for pickling. If you have a difficult time tracking down chile manzano, serrano chiles or cayenne peppers are great substitutions.

POBLANO: A mild, wide, heart-shaped dark green pepper, this chile is native to the state of Puebla, Mexico, and is included in many Mexican dishes. It's highly popular during Fiestas Patrias, the Mexican patriotic season. Because their skin is so thick, these chiles make great stuffing vessels and are strong enough to be easily handled when roasting, peeling, and dredging. They're perfect for *chiles en nogada*, *chiles rellenos* (page 142), and creamy *rajas poblanas* (page 118). Chiles poblanos are available in most supermarkets year-round, but Anaheim chiles make a good substitute if poblanos aren't available.

ANAHEIM: Native to New Mexico, these long, slender light green chiles make a great substitute for poblano chiles and are a slightly hotter substitute for bell peppers. They're also known as the California chile, the Magdalena chile, or simply just chile verde—they're ubiquitous. Anaheim peppers are perfect for roasting, adding to a potato stew, or eating grilled and wrapped in a corn tortilla with a piece of queso fresco.

HABANERO: The habanero is a seriously hot chile with a smoky, citrus-like taste. Although it hails from South America, this fiery chile is commonly used in the Yucatán Peninsula. It's popular in hot sauces, dry rubs, and powders and is great for pickling and making into a spicy salsa too.

SERRANO: Named after the *sierras* (mountain regions) of the Mexican states of Puebla and Hidalgo, the serrano chile is smaller than a jalapeño but brighter and spicier with a more flavorful zing. It's perfect for roasting; making into pico de gallo, hot sauces, and salsas; and even eating raw. Serrano chiles are as common as the jalapeño and can be found in most supermarkets.

JALAPEÑO: The jalapeño is named after the city of Xalapa (Jalapa), the capital of Veracruz, where the chile originates from. It is also known as *chile cuaresmeño*. Easy to grow and with a tolerant medium heat, the jalapeño is by far one of the favorites. Its flesh is thick, which makes it easy to stuff. It's delicious roasted and eaten raw. It adds spice to mild soups and stews and is always perfect for any kind of salsa and hot sauce.

RED JALAPEÑO: Red jalapeños are jalapeños left on the plant to ripen and mature. Their color shifts from green to red with time. While on the plant, their capsaicin (the chemical that's responsible for chile hotness) intensifies; their heat may escalate to the level of a serrano, and their flavor may sweeten. Red jalapeños are perfect for citrusy salsas and hot sauces. They make a great garnish as well.

HOW TO ROAST AND PEEL POBLANO CHILES

Poblanos taste best roasted over an open flame. Roasting simplifies the removal of the thin outer skin and gives them that wonderful, rich, smoky taste distinct in Mexican dishes. Poblanos can also be roasted in the oven or on the grill. My personal preference is over the stove burner. I find that I have more control of keeping the chiles from burning by using metal tongs and turning them during the roasting process.

Roasting Over a Stove Burner

1   Rinse poblano chiles and wipe dry with a paper towel. Lightly cover with olive oil (about ¼ teaspoon per chile). Rub thoroughly and wipe off any excess.

2   Turn stove burner on high. Using metal tongs, place 1 or 2 poblano chiles on burner, directly over the flame. You will begin to hear a crackling and popping sound. That is a good sound! It means the chile skins are blistering and separating from the chile.

3   Using metal tongs, turn the chiles every 2 to 3 minutes. Allow the skin to blacken on all sides, but do not let the skin turn to ash.

4   Carefully remove the charred chiles with tongs and place them in a clean plastic bag. Seal the bag or fold the opening over, leaving some air inside. This will allow the chiles to steam. Steam for at least 10 minutes.

5   Carefully open the plastic bag to release hot steam. When the chiles are cool enough to handle, remove them from the bag.

6   Place steamed chiles on a cutting board. Holding the chile by the stem and using the back of a knife or edge of a spoon, scrape the charred skin away from you.

7   If making chiles rellenos, make a vertical slit with a small knife about half an inch from the bottom tip of each chile to half an inch from the stem. Using a small spoon, carefully scrape and scoop out veins and as many seeds as you can.

8   If making rajas (chile strips) or another recipe that does not require a whole chile, cut each chile from the top (stem side) to the bottom. Cut off stem and cluster of seeds and scrape off veins and any extra seeds. Now the poblano chile is ready to be sliced or chopped and added to your recipe.

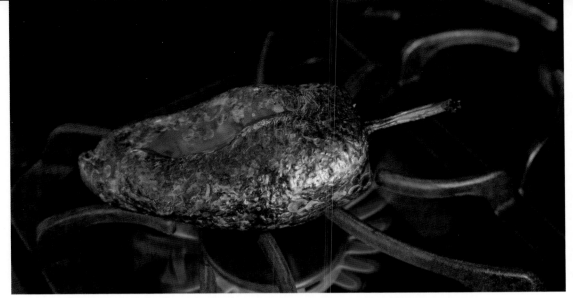

HOW TO CUT AND COOK NOPALES (CACTUS)

Cactus is one of my favorite vegetables because it has many health benefits. When cooked correctly, cactus is delicious and can be incorporated in meals in many different ways.

Many Latin markets sell cactus pads with the thorns already removed and sometimes even prechopped. If you purchase them with the thorns removed, they need to be cooked in the next couple of days, or they will begin to oxidize. When exposed to the air, the cut surface will darken, similar to cut apples or peaches.

If you don't plan to cook your cacti right away, I recommend purchasing them with thorns. They will keep fresh refrigerated for a few more days.

Removing Cactus Thorns

1   Using a kitchen towel, hold cactus pad flat on a cutting board. With a sharp knife, carefully cut along the side, around the edge, to remove any side thorns.

2   Scrape the cactus pad with a knife against the growth of the thorns and away from you. Carefully turn the pad to the other side and repeat. Slice off any dark, oxidized, or damaged areas.

3   When all thorns have been removed, rinse cactus with cold water and pat dry. Cut off and discard the base (approximately half an inch). Now the cactus pad is ready to be chopped or sliced.

Cooking Cactus for Recipes in this Book

3 pounds cactus, thorns removed, chopped

1 cup fresh cilantro sprigs

2 garlic cloves

¼ white onion

1 teaspoon salt

4   Place all ingredients in a large pot with lid. Heat covered over medium-low heat for 30 minutes, stirring a few times to combine all ingredients.

5   Remove lid and cook 10 minutes. Cactus will release liquid and boil rapidly.

6   Remove and discard cilantro, garlic, and onion. Drain, rinse, and let cactus cool completely before storing in a glass container with lid. Cooked cactus will keep approximately 5 days.

Tortillas

TORTILLAS DE MAÍZ
Corn Tortillas

The key to making soft corn tortillas is letting the masa rest. This allows it to absorb moisture and avoid drying out during the cooking process. I like to press an epazote leaf on the center to give them a little hint of its flavor. You can also use fresh cilantro or basil if you prefer. This is completely optional. To make the tortillas, you'll need a tortilla press, a comal (griddle), and two sheets of plastic; you can use a gallon-sized plastic freezer bag cut in half for the plastic.

PREPARATION TIME: 10 MINUTES
REST TIME: 90 MINUTES
COOK TIME: 40 MINUTES
MAKES 16

2½ cups masa harina (corn flour)

2¼ cups warm water

16 epazote leaves, rinsed (optional)

vegetable oil for brushing

1   Combine masa harina and water in a large bowl. Knead with hands until water has been completely absorbed and is no longer sticky. If masa begins to dry, add warm water a tablespoon at a time. Cover with plastic wrap or kitchen towel and let rest for 90 minutes.

2   Preheat comal over medium-high heat. Lightly brush with vegetable oil, then wipe with paper towel.

3   Knead dough again and make approximately 16 (2-inch) masa balls (50 grams each). Keep them in the bowl covered with plastic wrap or kitchen towel to avoid drying out.

4   Lay one piece of plastic on the surface of the tortilla press. Place a masa ball on the center and an epazote leaf over the ball (optional). Place the other piece of plastic over the masa ball and flatten gently to approximately 4½ inches in diameter.

5   Carefully remove plastic from each side of the tortilla and gently lay tortilla on hot comal. Cook for 30 seconds or until edges begin to change color slightly. Flip tortilla to other side and cook for 90 seconds. Flip a second time, to the original side. Tap the tortilla gently in the center; this will cause it to puff and cook with steam inside. Cook for 30 seconds. Place cooked tortillas in a clean folded kitchen towel or tortillero to keep warm. Repeat with remaining masa balls.

6   Serve immediately or store in a sealed plastic bag in the refrigerator.

TORTILLAS DE HARINA
Flour Tortillas

My definition of heaven was when my mom would slather butter on a freshly made tortilla de harina, roll it between her hands, and hand it to me to enjoy. Now I get to do the exact same thing with my son, and he looks forward to it every time, just like I did.

My recipe doesn't include lard or vegetable shortening; butter and milk give the tortillas that softness and buttery flavor. Just like with corn tortillas, the trick to keep them soft and pliable is the resting process to allow the ingredients to hydrate with the milk. Please don't skip that very important step.

PREPARATION TIME: 30 MINUTES
REST TIME: 15 MINUTES
COOK TIME: 15 MINUTES
MAKES 8

2 cups all-purpose flour plus more for dusting
1 teaspoon salt
½ teaspoon baking powder

¼ cup butter, melted and cooled to room temperature
1 cup hot milk

1   Whisk together flour, salt, and baking powder in a large bowl. Stir in butter and milk.

2   Knead dough with hands until dough is smooth and elastic and does not stick to hands, about 10 minutes.

3   Divide dough into 8 balls. Place in bowl and cover with a towel. Let dough rest for 15 minutes.

4   Lightly dust working surface and rolling pin with flour. Roll each ball of dough into an 8-inch tortilla. Place each uncooked tortilla on a platter covered with a kitchen towel to avoid drying out.

5   Heat comal (griddle) over medium heat. Cook each tortilla for 30 seconds on each side until golden-brown spots form. If tortilla puffs up, gently press down with a spatula to release hot steam. Place cooked tortillas in a clean folded kitchen towel or tortillero to keep warm.

6   Serve immediately or store in a sealed plastic bag in the refrigerator.

Salsas

SALSA MOLCAJETEADA

Molcajete Salsa

Every morning around breakfast time, you will find a large glass container of molcajete salsa on our kitchen table. I usually make this salsa on the weekend to have ready for the week's breakfast eggs. It's chunky, has the right amount of spice, and makes our breakfast a hundred times better.

If the thought of using a molcajete (mortar and pestle) is intimidating to you, this is the perfect recipe to get you started. If a molcajete is not available, don't let that stop you from making this salsa. Use a blender or food processor on the pulse setting to get this salsa's chunky consistency.

PREPARATION TIME: 10 MINUTES
COOK TIME: 15 MINUTES
MAKES 2 CUPS

3 garlic cloves, husks on
4 jalapeños
⅓ white onion

5 Roma tomatoes, stem scar sliced off
3 tomatillos, husked, stem scar sliced off
1 teaspoon salt or to taste

1   Place garlic, jalapeños, onion, tomatoes, and tomatillos on a comal or skillet over medium-high heat. Remove garlic after 3–4 minutes, once the husks can be easily removed. Continue roasting other ingredients, turning frequently with tongs, until charred spots form, about 6 more minutes. Do not over roast. You should still be able to see some fresh areas.

2   While vegetables finish roasting, remove garlic husks and place garlic cloves in molcajete. Add salt. Grind garlic to a paste.

3   Once vegetables have finished roasting, transfer jalapeños to molcajete and grind. Remove and discard stems as they detach during the grinding process.

4   Add onion. Continue grinding until onion is in small pieces and almost paste-like.

5   Grind tomatoes and tomatillos last, mixing and pressing salsa until desired consistency.

SALSA MACHA
Salsa for the Brave Ones

When visiting my mother in El Paso, we always take a day trip to Las Cruces, New Mexico. We like to visit Old Mesilla, enjoy some New Mexican food, and make some purchases at their local fudge shop. Driving back, however, I always make it a point to look for roadside vendors. Last time I visited, I purchased a burlap bundle filled with pine nuts and a large bag of these beautiful dried puya chiles from one of the vendors. All I could think about was adding them to a salsa macha.

Salsa macha translates to "the salsa for the brave ones," for obvious reasons. It packs a punch. Its main spicy ingredient is dried red arbol chile. In my recipe, I added puya chiles as well. Puya can be found in the spice or produce section of your Latin grocery store. It can also be found online. You can also use dried chipotle chiles, guajillo chiles, or even throw in some fresh jalapeño or serrano chile slices once the sauce has been processed.

Salsa macha is versatile. It can be used to spice up soups and stews, added to your tacos or morning eggs, and even scooped up with corn chips and tortillas.

PREPARATION TIME: 10 MINUTES
COOK TIME: 20 MINUTES
MAKES 1¾ CUPS

3 tablespoons raw pepitas

3 tablespoons sesame seeds

1¼ cup olive oil

¼ white onion, roughly chopped

3 garlic cloves

1 corn tortilla

½ cup dried arbol chiles, tops removed

½ cup dried puya chiles, tops removed

1 teaspoon salt

1   Heat a medium skillet over medium heat. Add pepitas and toast, stirring frequently until golden, about 4 minutes. Transfer to a medium bowl and set aside.

2   Decrease heat to medium-low. Add sesame seeds to skillet. Stir frequently until slightly golden brown, about 2 minutes. Transfer to bowl.

3   Heat oil in skillet over medium heat. Add onion and garlic. Fry evenly for 1 minute, turning with tongs. Transfer to bowl.

4   Add corn tortilla to skillet and fry until crispy. Do not burn. Transfer to bowl.

5   Add dried arbol chiles and puya chiles to skillet in batches. Fry each batch for 30 seconds to 1 minute or until their color darkens. Transfer to bowl. Set oil aside to cool completely.

6   Once oil is cool, transfer oil plus everything in bowl to a food processor or blender. Add salt and pulse to a coarse, chunky consistency.

7   Transfer to glass jar with lid. Store sealed in the refrigerator up to 6 months.

SALSA DE CHILE DE ÁRBOL

Chile de Arbol Salsa

There is no right or wrong way to prepare chile de arbol salsa. I make it just like my mom taught me and fry the dried chiles prior to boiling, giving them a roasted feel. This salsa is a favorite among taco connoisseurs because it packs a very spicy kick. If your salsa is too spicy, add an extra tomato or two.

PREPARATION TIME: 25 MINUTES
COOK TIME: 15 MINUTES
MAKES 2 ¼ CUPS

30 dried arbol chiles

1 dried guajillo chile

2 tablespoons vegetable oil

2 garlic cloves

2 Roma tomatoes, halved lengthwise

¼ white onion

¾ teaspoon salt

½ cup chopped fresh cilantro

1   Place dried chiles in a large strainer. Rinse with cold water and transfer to a paper towel to dry. Remove stems.

2   Heat oil in a large sauté pan over medium heat. Add dried chiles and fry for 3 minutes, stirring frequently.

3   Transfer fried chiles to a large saucepan with 2 cups water. Do not throw away oil. Heat chiles over medium-low heat. Boil for 5 minutes. Remove saucepan from heat and cover.

4   While chiles boil, place garlic cloves, tomatoes, and onion in oil chiles fried in. Fry evenly for 5 minutes, turning frequently with tongs. Transfer to saucepan with chiles and let soak for 20 minutes or until chile skins are soft.

5   Transfer everything in saucepan to blender. Add salt and blend until smooth. Run through a strainer if needed.

6   Transfer salsa to a serving bowl. Stir in cilantro. Serve.

CEBOLLAS ENCURTIDAS CON HABANERO

Habanero-Spiced Pickled Onions

Add a little bit of tang, crunch, and heat to your meals with these mouth-watering habanero-spiced pickled onions. Perfect on your favorite tacos and breakfast egg dishes, these bright pink strips of spicy onion are incredibly easy to prepare. Add more habaneros to turn up the heat, or omit them completely for a more peppery feel.

PREPARATION TIME: 10 MINUTES
COOK TIME: 10 MINUTES
COOL TIME: 45 MINUTES
SERVES 10

1 large red onion, thinly sliced (about 2 cups)

1–2 habanero chiles

2 garlic cloves

2 cups white vinegar

¼ cup granulated sugar

½ teaspoon salt

2 teaspoons black peppercorns

1   Place onion, habaneros, and garlic in a large jar with lid. Set aside.

2   Place vinegar, sugar, salt, and peppercorns in a medium saucepan over medium heat. When mixture starts to boil, carefully pour mixture into jar with onion, habaneros, and garlic. Press onions down with a spoon to make sure they are submerged under the liquid. Set aside for 45 minutes or until cooled.

3   Serve or store tightly sealed in refrigerator.

SALSA BORRACHA

Drunken Salsa

I've tasted so many variations of salsa borracha. Some are made with dried pasilla chiles; others, like mine, are made with fresh jalapeños, serrano chiles, Roma tomatoes, and onion. One thing is for sure—they all have beer as a main ingredient. You can use dark or light beer, your preference. The flavor is rich as the alcohol evaporates in the cooking process. Serve this salsa to accompany your favorite taco, or scoop it up with corn tostadas.

PREPARATION TIME: 5 MINUTES
COOK TIME: 30 MINUTES
SERVES 4–6

2 large jalapeños, tops removed, chopped in large pieces

2 serrano chiles, tops removed, chopped in large pieces

3 Roma tomatoes, stem scar sliced off

I cup roughly chopped white onion

2 garlic cloves, husks on

I tablespoon olive oil

I teaspoon sea salt

I cup dark or light beer

tostadas or corn tortillas for serving

1   Heat large skillet or comal over medium-high heat. Add chiles, tomatoes, onion, and garlic. Cook until charred spots form, about 10 minutes, turning frequently with tongs. Remove from heat and carefully remove husks from garlic cloves.

2   Heat olive oil in a medium saucepan. Add roasted vegetables and season with salt. Cook for 10 minutes or until vegetables release liquid.

3   Using a potato or bean masher, mash the larger vegetable pieces into a chunky salsa consistency.

4   Add beer and cook for 7–10 minutes or until salsa thickens.

5   Serve with tostadas or tortillas.

SALSA VERDE

Green Salsa

This salsa verde is my go-to salsa for enchiladas, chilaquiles, and any stew that needs a little bit of tomatillo tang. It's great for making ahead of time and freezing for when you're not quite sure what to make for dinner or when you are in the mood for chips and salsa.

PREPARATION TIME: 10 MINUTES
COOK TIME: 20 MINUTES
MAKES 4 CUPS

12 tomatillos, husked and rinsed

2 large jalapeños, stems removed

2 large serrano chiles, stems removed

½ cup roughly chopped white onion

2 garlic cloves

1 teaspoon salt

½ cup chopped fresh cilantro

1   Boil 6 cups water in a large saucepan over medium heat. Add tomatillos, jalapeños, and serranos. Remove tomatillos when they darken, about 8 minutes. Continue boiling the chiles for 8–10 minutes more. Do not throw away water.

2   Place tomatillos, chiles, onion, garlic, salt, and 1 cup chile water in a blender. Pulse until desired consistency.

3   Transfer to a large salsa bowl and stir in cilantro. To store, place salsa in a large jar or container with lid and keep refrigerated.

PICO DE GALLO CON PIÑA

Pineapple Pico de Gallo

This pico de gallo is not your typical pico de gallo. With the addition of sweet pineapple chunks to the mix, this colorful classic is a delicious way to dress up any street food–style dish where you want a sweet-and-spicy feel. It's my favorite salsa to serve during summer cookouts.

PREPARATION TIME: 10 MINUTES
SERVES 4–6

1 cup chopped pineapple

1 ½ cups chopped Roma tomato

½ cup chopped white onion

1 jalapeño, chopped

¼ cup (packed) chopped cilantro

½ teaspoon salt

2 tablespoons lime juice

1   Place all ingredients in a medium bowl. Toss to combine. Serve.

ESCABECHE DE VERDURAS

Vegetable Escabeche

My mom had a tall olive-green Tupperware container in the back of the refrigerator specifically made to store pickles. It had a long handle attached to a strainer to pull up the pickles without making a mess. She loved that container because she used it to store her escabeche. Every morning, noon, and night, she took the container out of the refrigerator and set it on the kitchen table. She happily lifted the handle and took a pickled jalapeño, a few slices of carrot, and some onion and placed them next to the meal she was about to enjoy. I didn't understand her fascination back then until I started pickling my own vegetables. Now I have the same routine.

If you're looking to add a bit of spice to your meals, this vegetable escabeche goes with just about any Mexican meal. To make it, I use manzano chiles. Don't let their yellow color and apple-like shape fool you. These peppers can be twice as hot as the jalapeño. Manzano chiles can be found in the produce section of any Latin store or online. You can also use jalapeños or habanero chiles as a replacement in this recipe.

PREPARATION TIME: 10 MINUTES
COOK TIME: 20 MINUTES
MAKES 6 CUPS

1 cup distilled white vinegar

½ cup vegetable oil

¼ white onion, sliced

¼ red onion, sliced

6 garlic cloves

2 large carrots, sliced (about 2 cups)

4 manzano chiles, chopped (about 2½ cups)

3 cactus pads, sliced (about 3 cups)

2 cups cauliflower florets

3 dried bay leaves

1 teaspoon dried Mexican oregano, crushed

1 teaspoon salt

1   Combine 2 cups water and vinegar in a large saucepan. Heat over medium-low heat and bring to a boil.

2   While water and vinegar come to a boil, heat oil in a large frying pan over medium heat. Lightly fry white and red onion and garlic cloves, stirring frequently, about 2 minutes. Transfer to a paper towel–lined plate. Set aside.

3   Using the same frying pan and oil, fry carrots and manzano chiles for 3 minutes. Transfer to paper towel–lined plate.

4   When the water and vinegar boil, add cactus, cauliflower, and fried carrots. Boil for 5 minutes or until cactus darkens in color.

5   Add manzano chiles, fried onions and garlic, bay leaves, oregano, and salt to boiling liquid. Stir to mix well for 1 minute. Remove from heat and let cool completely.

6   Serve or store in the refrigerator in a tightly sealed glass jar.

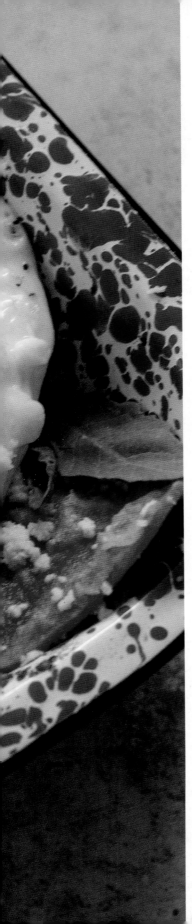

Desayuno
(Breakfast)

DESAYUNO DE PUDIN DE CHIA

Breakfast Chia Pudding

This chia pudding is my go-to rush-out-the-door breakfast. Filled with seasonal fruit, nuts, and seeds, this is a breakfast I don't mind enjoying while stuck in Los Angeles traffic. Prep the night before and just add your favorite toppings the next morning. It will keep you satisfied and full until the next meal with absolutely no guilt.

PREPARATION TIME: 5 MINUTES
CHILL TIME: OVERNIGHT
SERVES 2

¼ cup chia seeds

1 cup milk (regular or plant-based) plus more for serving

½ cup plain yogurt (2% fat or plant-based)

1 ½ tablespoons maple syrup

1 teaspoon vanilla extract

TOPPINGS

blackberries

banana slices

sliced almonds

raw pepitas

brown sugar

1   Combine chia seeds, milk, yogurt, maple syrup, and vanilla in a medium bowl. Stir. Cover and refrigerate overnight.

2   When ready to eat, divide chia mixture between 2 bowls or cups. Stir in 2 to 3 tablespoons milk (optional). Top with blackberries, banana, almonds, pepitas, and brown sugar. Enjoy.

HUEVOS EN PURGATORIO

Purgatory Eggs

Purgatory eggs—eggs cooked in a tomato-rich, pequin-spiced salsa and topped with gooey melted cheese—are a favorite brunch meal of mine. This casual dish is customarily enjoyed family style and scooped up with bolillo bread. Silverware is optional, but have plenty of napkins on hand.

PREPARATION TIME: 10 MINUTES
COOK TIME: 20 MINUTES
SERVES 4

1 teaspoon canola oil

1 garlic clove, chopped

½ cup chopped white onion

4–6 dried pequin chiles

3 Roma tomatoes, finely chopped

½ teaspoon salt

3 large eggs

1 cup shredded mozzarella cheese

¼ teaspoon black pepper

bolillo bread for serving

1   Heat oil over medium heat in large saucepan. Add garlic and onion. Cook 2 minutes or until onion is translucent.

2   Stir in pequin chiles, tomatoes, and salt. Continue cooking for 10 minutes or until mixture thickens and tomatoes release liquid.

3   Gently crack eggs into mixture, making sure yolks stay intact. Sprinkle with cheese and pepper. Cover and let cheese melt and eggs set (to your preference) for at least 2 minutes.

4   Remove from heat. Serve family style with bolillos.

HUEVOS PERDIDOS CON EJOTES

Lost Eggs with Green Beans

Huevos perdidos literally means "lost eggs." These eggs get "lost" in a rich and spicy chile de arbol and guajillo sauce, accompanied by cooked green beans. Besides green beans, this recipe can take an entire new flavor when cooked with nopales (see page 15). If you love a spicy breakfast, I think you will love this one. Don't forget the beans and tortillas!

PREPARATION TIME: 15 MINUTES
COOK TIME: 30 MINUTES
SERVES 6

12 ounces green beans, tips removed, chopped

2 tablespoons cooking oil, divided

½ white onion, divided

10 dried guajillo chiles, stems and seeds removed

4 dried arbol chiles, stems and seeds removed

1 teaspoon garlic powder

½ teaspoon ground cumin

1 teaspoon salt

6 eggs

1   Bring 6 cups water to a boil. Add green beans and boil for 8 minutes. Drain and set aside.

2   Heat 1 tablespoon oil in a large sauté pan. Add ¼ piece onion, in large chunks, and dried chiles. Fry for 4 minutes.

3   Add 3 cups water, garlic powder, ground cumin, and salt. Cook for 10 minutes.

4   Carefully transfer hydrated chiles, onion, and water they cooked in to a blender. Remove the center cap from the lid of the blender and place a towel over it to prevent any pressure from building and hot liquid from spilling. Starting with the lowest speed and gradually increasing, blend until smooth. Run through a mesh strainer into a large bowl, pressing and scraping the liquid out. Discard chiles and onion.

5   Return sauce mixture to blender and add eggs. Blend for 30 seconds or until eggs are completely mixed in with the sauce.

6   Chop the remaining ¼ piece onion into small pieces. Heat remaining tablespoon oil in the same sauté pan used to hydrate chiles over medium heat. Add onion. Cook for 1 minute.

7   Add green beans. Fry for 3 minutes, stirring frequently.

8   Add sauce mixture and stir slowly, folding ingredients constantly until eggs begin to set, about 5 minutes. The mixture should resemble cooked chorizo or ground beef.

9   Serve with refried beans and flour tortillas.

ENFRIJOLADAS DE QUESO

Cheese Enfrijoladas

Many delicious dishes can be prepared with leftover beans. This is my—and a crowd—favorite. A savory smooth and creamy sauce drenches tortillas wrapped over delicious queso fresco. If pinto beans are not available, try this recipe with black beans. If preparing it for kids, omit the serrano chile for a much milder version.

PREPARATION TIME: 15 MINUTES
COOK TIME: 40 MINUTES
SERVES 6

1½ cups cooked pinto beans
   (page 121)

2 cups water beans cooked in
   or 2 cups water with a
   pinch of salt

¼ white onion plus 1 tablespoon,
   all roughly chopped, divided

1 large Roma tomato,
   roughly chopped

1 small serrano chile, seeds and
   veins removed

2 garlic cloves

3 tablespoons cooking oil, divided

2 large fresh epazote leaves

12 corn tortillas

2½ cups shredded queso fresco

TOPPINGS

sour cream or Mexican crema

crumbled queso fresco

sliced red onion

epazote leaves

sliced avocado

1   Combine beans, water beans were cooked in, ¼ onion, tomato, serrano chile, and garlic cloves in a blender. Blend until smooth.

2   Heat 2 tablespoons oil in a large saucepan over medium heat. Add remaining tablespoon chopped onion and fry for 2 minutes, stirring frequently. Do not burn.

3   Reduce heat to medium-low. Discard fried onion and pour in bean mixture. Add epazote leaves and cover. Cook for 20 minutes, stirring frequently. Discard epazote leaves. Keep mixture warm.

4   While bean mixture cooks, heat remaining tablespoon oil in a large frying pan over medium heat. Lightly fry each tortilla for 15 seconds on each side. Stack on a separate plate and keep warm.

5   Dip tortillas in bean mixture and fill each with 3 tablespoons cheese. Roll and arrange seam side down in a casserole dish.

6   Pour remaining bean sauce over rolled tortillas. Serve. Garnish with toppings.

CHILAQUILES ROJOS
Red Chilaquiles

I tend to prepare a large batch of this red chilaquil sauce ahead of time. Some I freeze, and the rest I have ready for when I have breakfast guests over. These are a hit. The tomatillos' tangy taste complements the red chile heat nicely. Keep the tortilla chips separate from the sauce until ready to serve to keep their delicate crisp intact.

PREPARATION TIME: 15 MINUTES
COOK TIME: 55 MINUTES
SERVES 4

1 cup plus 1 tablespoon vegetable oil, divided

12 (6-inch) corn tortillas, sliced in triangles

8 guajillo chiles, stems and seeds removed, wiped clean

5 arbol chiles, stems and seeds removed, wiped clean

4 tomatillos

2½ cups vegetable broth, chicken broth, or water, divided

3 garlic cloves

¼ teaspoon whole cumin

¼ teaspoon dried oregano

¼ white onion plus a few slices for garnish

½ teaspoon salt or to taste

2 epazote sprigs plus more leaves for garnish

½ cup crumbled queso fresco

3–4 fried eggs

black pepper

1   Heat 1 cup oil in a large skillet over medium heat. Add tortilla pieces a few at a time and fry evenly, about 45 seconds on each side or until golden. Transfer to a paper towel–lined dish to drain any extra oil.

2   Bring 4 cups water to a boil. Add chiles. Boil 2 minutes. Add tomatillos and continue boiling until tomatillo color darkens, about 3 minutes. Remove tomatillos (save for later), turn heat off, and let chiles continue hydrating for about 5 minutes.

3   Transfer chiles to a blender. Add 1 cup broth (or water) and blend until smooth. Run sauce through a strainer and set aside. Rinse blender container.

4   Place 1 cup broth (or water), tomatillos, garlic, cumin, and oregano in blender. Blend until smooth.

5   Heat remaining tablespoon oil in a sauté pan over medium heat. Add ¼ piece onion and fry for 3 minutes. Remove onion with tongs and discard.

6   Add tomatillo sauce to pan. Cook for 6 minutes.

7   Slowly add the chile sauce. Stir in salt and cook for 10 minutes.

8   Add remaining ½ cup broth (or water) and epazote sprigs. Cook for 15 minutes.

9   Quickly toss tortilla chips in sauce as they are served. Top with onion slices, epazote leaves, queso fresco, eggs, and a sprinkle of pepper.

CHILAQUILES VERDES
Green Chilaquiles

One of my favorite uses for the salsa verde in this book is for making these green chilaquiles as a Sunday brunch dish. They're spicy, they're tangy, and they have just the right amount of crisp. Top them with your favorite protein and garnish with radish slices, red onion, and avocado. Don't forget the crema and queso fresco—they are a must!

PREPARATION TIME: 10 MINUTES
COOK TIME: 15 MINUTES
SERVES 4

1 cup plus 1 tablespoon vegetable oil

8 (6-inch) corn tortillas, sliced in triangles

2 cups salsa verde (page 34)

TOPPINGS

crumbled queso fresco

Mexican crema

4 radishes, thinly sliced

¼ cup sliced red onion

1 large avocado, sliced

2 tablespoons fresh cilantro leaves

1   Heat 1 cup oil in a large skillet over medium heat. Add tortilla pieces a few at a time and fry evenly, about 45 seconds on each side or until golden. Transfer to a paper towel–lined dish to drain any extra oil.

2   Heat remaining tablespoon oil in a large sauté pan over medium heat. Add salsa verde and 1 cup water. Cook 10 minutes, stirring slowly. Remove from heat.

3   Fold in tortilla chips, lightly coating with sauce. Serve. Sprinkle with queso fresco and top with Mexican crema, radishes, red onion, avocado, and cilantro.

Botanas
(Appetizers)

PANELA AL HORNO CON NOPALES

Baked Panela with Cactus

When baked, panela cheese does not melt but softens. It can still be sliced. When topped with spicy nopales during the baking process and served with tostadas, it turns into the most delicious appetizer. Wrap the slices with warm corn or flour tortillas and you will have a complete taco spread.

PREPARATION TIME: 10 MINUTES
COOK TIME: 21 MINUTES
SERVES 6

1 tablespoon olive oil

½ cup chopped white onion

1 garlic clove, chopped

3 dried arbol chiles, tops and seeds removed, chopped

6 cactus pads, chopped and cooked (page 15)

¾ cup chopped cilantro

1 (10-ounce) panela cheese wheel

warm corn tortillas or tostadas for serving

1   Preheat oven to 350 degrees.

2   Heat oil in a large pan over medium heat. Add chopped onion. Cook for 4 minutes.

3   Add garlic and arbol chiles. Fry for 2 minutes, stirring frequently.

4   Remove from heat. Add cooked cactus and chopped cilantro.

5   Place panela cheese on a small ovenproof dish. Spoon cactus mixture over cheese. Bake for 15 minutes or until cheese is soft.

6   Serve with corn tortillas or tostadas.

NACHOS CON CAMARONES Y PICO DE GALLO

Shrimp Nachos with Pico de Gallo

These shrimp nachos with pico de gallo are what I call fun on a platter. Not only are these nachos colorful and festive, but they are also delicious and fun to share. We consider them our fun food of choice when tailgating and a popular party food when friends and neighbors drop by. For milder nachos, substitute the chipotle powder with paprika. If you make the pico de gallo first, it can chill while you make the nachos.

PREPARATION TIME: 10 MINUTES
COOK TIME: 15 MINUTES
CHILL TIME: 30 MINUTES
SERVES 12

Shrimp Nachos

- 1 tablespoon butter
- 1 pound medium shrimp, peeled and deveined
- ½ teaspoon garlic salt
- ½ teaspoon chipotle powder or paprika
- 6 cups corn chips

- 3 cups shredded Monterey Jack cheese
- 1 (11-ounce) package of Mexican (pork, beef, or soy) chorizo, cooked
- 1 cup cooked pinto beans, drained (page 121)

TOPPINGS

sour cream
pico de gallo
avocado slices
fresh cilantro sprigs

1   Preheat oven to 425 degrees.

2   Melt butter in a large sauté pan over medium heat. Add shrimp and season with garlic salt. Cook for 3–4 minutes or until shrimp turn pink. Sprinkle with chipotle powder (or paprika), stir, and remove from heat. Keep warm.

3   Arrange corn chips on a large baking tray. Layer with cheese. Top with chorizo and beans. Bake for 5–7 minutes or until cheese melts. Remove from oven.

4   Top chips with shrimp, sour cream, pico de gallo, avocado, and cilantro. Serve immediately.

Pico de Gallo

- 1 large Roma tomato, cubed
- ½ cup chopped white onion
- 1 large jalapeño or 2 serrano chiles, chopped

- 1 tablespoon lime juice
- 2 tablespoons chopped fresh cilantro
- salt to taste

1   Combine all ingredients in a medium bowl. Stir to mix well. Cover. Refrigerate for at least 30 minutes before serving.

ESQUITE FRITO
Fried Esquite

The word *esquite* derives from the Nahuatl word *ízquitl*, which means "toasted." This popular Mexican street food is known by a variety of names. In Chihuahua, it is known as *elote en vaso* (corn in a cup); in the northeast region of Mexico, it's referred to as *toles*, *trolelotes*, or *coctel de elote* (corn cocktail); and in Aguascalientes, it's called *chascas*.

The base is always the same: corn, salt, and epazote. Many variations include frying with arbol chile and topping with cotija cheese, mayonnaise, chile powder, a very hot sauce, and a sprinkle of lime juice. My version includes pequin chiles, onion, and butter.

PREPARATION TIME: 10 MINUTES
COOK TIME: 28 MINUTES
SERVES 6

5 cups white corn

1½ teaspoons salt, divided

3 tablespoons butter

¾ cup finely chopped white onion

30 dried pequin chiles, finely chopped

1–2 epazote sprigs

TOPPINGS

lime juice

crumbled cotija cheese

chile powder

hot sauce

mayonnaise

1   Combine corn kernels, 1 teaspoon salt, and 6 cups water in a large saucepan over medium heat. Boil for 15 minutes. Reserve ½ cup water. Drain the rest and set aside.

2   Melt butter in a large sauté pan over medium heat. Add onions and cook until tender, about 3 minutes.

3   Add corn, pequin chiles, epazote sprigs, remaining ½ teaspoon salt, and reserved ½ cup water. Cover. Reduce heat to medium-low and cook for 10 minutes.

4   Serve. Top with lime juice, cotija cheese, chile powder or hot sauce, and mayonnaise.

GUACAMOLE
Classic Guacamole

Nothing beats the classic flavors of a perfectly balanced guacamole. This recipe has the right amount of spice and citrus tang to pair with a bowl of tortilla chips or as a topping to your *garnachas*. The secret to its chunky texture is to gently mash with a fork or molcajete and tejolote (see page 7).

PREPARATION TIME: 10 MINUTES
SERVES 4

2 large avocados, pitted and peeled (about 2 cups)

½ teaspoon sea salt

2 tablespoons lime juice

1 large Roma tomato, finely chopped (about 1 cup)

1 large serrano chile, seeds removed, finely chopped

1 jalapeño, seeds removed, finely chopped

½ cup chopped white onion

¼ cup chopped fresh cilantro

corn tortilla chips for serving

1   Combine avocado, salt, and lime juice in a serving dish or molcajete. Mash avocado with tejolote or fork, stirring to mix in salt and lime juice.

2   Add tomato, chiles, onion, and cilantro. Stir to mix all ingredients thoroughly.

3   Serve with corn tortilla chips.

GARBANZOS PICOSITOS

Spicy Garbanzo Beans

My husband is a big soccer fan. He loves to watch both Mexican soccer and European soccer games on Sundays. That also means that these spicy garbanzo beans will be at hand for him to snack on as he cheers on his favorite teams. These spicy garbanzo beans have a nice citrus kick and go nicely with a frosty beer.

PREPARATION TIME: 10 MINUTES
COOK TIME: 20 MINUTES
SERVES 2–4

1 teaspoon paprika

1 teaspoon garlic salt

¼ teaspoon ground black pepper

¼ teaspoon ground ginger

¼ teaspoon chipotle powder

⅛ teaspoon (pinch) ground cumin

2 tablespoons olive oil

1 (15-ounce) can garbanzo beans, drained and rinsed

1 tablespoon lime zest

1 tablespoon lime juice

1   Combine paprika, garlic salt, pepper, ginger, chipotle, and cumin in a small bowl. Stir to mix evenly. Set aside.

2   Heat oil in a large frying pan over medium heat. Add garbanzo beans. Fry evenly by stirring with a large spoon and shaking pan for about 15 minutes.

3   Sprinkle seasoning mix over garbanzo beans and stir to distribute evenly. Cook for 2 minutes.

4   Transfer beans to a paper towel–lined plate. Sprinkle with lime zest and lime juice. Serve immediately.

CEVICHE DE ELOTE

White Corn Ceviche

When salad season arrives, I like to prepare this hybrid salad-and-ceviche treat. It is a great complementary dish to any picnic food because it can be served as a side salad on hot days. Just like esquite (see page 61), this spicy corn ceviche conveniently travels well in a cup.

PREPARATION TIME: 15 MINUTES
CHILL TIME: 60 MINUTES
SERVES 8

4 cups white corn

4 green onions, chopped

1 cup chopped red bell pepper

2 serrano chiles, seeds and veins removed, finely chopped

4 radishes, sliced in matchsticks

½ cup chopped fresh cilantro

3 tablespoons olive oil

¼ cup lime juice

½ teaspoon salt

¼ teaspoon black pepper

1   Combine ingredients in a large bowl. Stir to combine. Refrigerate for 1 hour before serving.

AGUACHILE NEGRO

Black Aguachile

Fresh and spicy is what comes to mind when enjoying this variation of aguachile. The dark and savory citrus marinade is what gives this popular dish from Sinaloa a distinct taste. Enjoy it with tostadas or salty crackers. Don't forget to top it off with a big chunk of creamy avocado.

PREPARATION TIME: 30 MINUTES
SERVES 8

I pound medium raw shrimp, peeled, deveined, and butterflied

1¼ cups lime juice, divided

I teaspoon sea salt

½ teaspoon ground black pepper

1½ tablespoons dried pequin chiles

I large garlic clove

¼ cup soy sauce

I tablespoon hot sauce

I teaspoon vegetable or shrimp bouillon

I tablespoon seasoning sauce (such as Jugo Maggi)

I tablespoon Worcestershire sauce

2 cups sliced cucumber

¼ red onion, sliced

⅓ cup fresh cilantro sprigs

½ avocado, sliced

corn chips, tostadas or crackers for serving

1   Combine shrimp, I cup lime juice, salt, and pepper in a large glass bowl. Stir to distribute ingredients. Set aside for shrimp to "cook" in lime juice for about 15 minutes.

2   Place pequin chiles and garlic clove in a large molcajete (mortar and pestle). Grind until a paste forms. Add soy sauce, hot sauce, bouillon, seasoning sauce, Worcestershire sauce, ¼ cup water, and remaining ¼ cup lime juice to molcajete. Stir to mix well.

3   Drain shrimp from their "cooking" liquid and transfer to molcajete mixture. Stir to mix well.

4   Top with cucumber slices, onion, cilantro, and avocado. Serve with corn chips, tostadas or crackers.

Ensaladas
(Salads)

ENSALADA DE NOPALITOS

Cactus Salad

"*Si te quedan babosos, lo estás haciendo mal.*" ("If they turn out slimy, you are doing it wrong.") That's what my mom used to tell me when she taught me how to cook cactus. "*Llama bajita, paciencia, y sin agua*" ("Low heat, patience, and no water") was the key to non-slimy cactus.

Now I've perfected the art of cooking cactus. Every Sunday I clean my pads of thorns and chop and cook them so they're ready for the week. I add them to fideo (page 87) and scrambled eggs, save them for tacos (page 133), or serve them up with a smoky red sauce (page 117). This salad is my favorite on hot afternoons. Served on tostadas or crackers, it's a complete meal.

PREPARATION TIME: 10 MINUTES
CHILL TIME: 1 HOUR
SERVES 6

3 pounds cooked cactus (page 15)

1 cup chopped Roma tomatoes

½ cup chopped white onion

1 large jalapeño, seeds and veins removed, chopped

¾ cup crumbled queso fresco

½ teaspoon salt

½ teaspoon dried oregano, crushed

1½ tablespoons extra-virgin olive oil

1   Fold together all ingredients in a large salad bowl. Refrigerate for 1 hour. Serve.

ENSALADA DE TUNA ROJA, NARANJA, Y HIERBABUENA

Red Prickly Pear, Orange, and Peppermint Salad

Every time I see prickly pears at the grocery store, I take a few home and prepare this delicious fruit salad. Paired with plump orange wedges and a drizzle of sweet honey syrup, this luscious treat is perfect as a sweet snack or something to enjoy first thing in the morning, after a workout, or as a light breakfast.

PREPARATION TIME: 15 MINUTES
SERVES 4

2 tablespoons honey

2 tablespoons lime juice

4 navel oranges

4 red prickly pears

2 tablespoons chopped fresh peppermint

1 Whisk together honey and lime juice in a small bowl. Set aside.

2 Peel oranges and separate wedges. Using a small knife, remove as much of the pith as possible. Place peeled wedges in a medium serving bowl.

3 Slice off both ends of each prickly pear. Make a vertical slit down the skin and pull to peel. Slice in half lengthwise (scoop out seeds if desired). Slice in wedges and arrange in serving bowl with orange wedges.

4 Pour honey and lime mixture evenly over fruit. Sprinkle with fresh mint.

GAZPACHO MORELIANO
Morelia Gazpacho

When the hot weather arrives, it's time to enjoy a refreshing combination of colors and flavors. Morelia's most famous fruit cocktail, *gazpacho Moreliano* (also spelled *gaspacho*), is a vibrant fruit mixture. Gazpacho vendors line the streets with colorful bowls of toppings for you to choose from. The gazpacho Moreliano base always consists of chopped jicama, pineapple, and mango. Onion, orange juice, lime juice, chili powder, and crumbled cotija cheese are also part of this mouthwatering treat. Many variations include watermelon, vinegar, and jalapeño. I like to add bits of cucumber to mine for extra flavor and color.

PREPARATION TIME: 15 MINUTES
SERVES 4

1 cup cubed jicama

1 cup cubed pineapple

1 cup cubed mango

1 cup cubed watermelon

1 cup peeled and cubed cucumber

¼ cup finely chopped onion

½ cup orange juice

3 tablespoons fresh lime juice

crumbled cotija cheese for serving

crushed dried pequin chile or chili powder
 for serving

1   Place jicama, fruit, cucumber, onion, orange juice, and lime juice in a large bowl. Toss to combine.

2   Serve in tall glasses. Top with cotija cheese and chile powder.

ENSALADA DE MANGO Y JÍCAMA CON ADEREZO PICOSO DE CILANTRO Y LIMA

Mango and Jicama Salad with Spicy Cilantro Lime Dressing

It's all about the dressing for this salad. It's tangy, garlicky, and spicy—a perfect complement to the mango sweetness and fresh crunch from the jicama and romaine. Serve it as a side salad or add your favorite protein to enjoy it as a main meal.

PREPARATION TIME: 20 MINUTES
SERVES 8

Mango and Jicama Salad

1 head romaine lettuce,
   torn into bite-sized pieces

3 large red mangos, cubed (about 2½ cups)

½ jicama, cut in thin strips (about 1½ cups)

spicy cilantro lime dressing

1   Combine ingredients in a large salad bowl. Add half the dressing and toss to distribute. Serve with remaining dressing on the side.

Spicy Cilantro Lime Dressing

MAKES 1½ CUPS

1 bunch fresh cilantro, roughly chopped
   (about 2 cups)

2 garlic cloves

⅓ cup lime juice

2 tablespoons distilled white vinegar

½ teaspoon dried oregano

1 serrano chile, vein and seeds removed,
   roughly chopped

½ teaspoon sea salt

⅓ cup extra virgin olive oil

1   Add cilantro, garlic, lime juice, vinegar, oregano, chile, and salt to a food processor. Pulse a few times. Add olive oil in a slow stream. Continue processing until ingredients have mixed well. Transfer to a serving dish or jar.

Sopas y Guisos

(Soups and Stews)

SOPA DE REPOLLO

Cabbage Soup

Every time my mom comes to visit, I ask her to make me a big batch of this cabbage soup. I save a good amount to eat throughout the week and freeze the rest in smaller portions to enjoy later. It's such a great soup because it's hearty, loaded with vegetables, and quick and easy to prepare when you are short on time.

PREPARATION TIME: 10 MINUTES
COOK TIME: 30 MINUTES
SERVES 8–10

½ head cabbage, chopped (4 cups)

1 cup chopped carrots

1 cup chopped celery

2 cups chopped chayote squash

1 tablespoon olive oil

½ cup chopped white onion

1 garlic clove, chopped

1 (8-ounce) can low sodium tomato sauce

1½ tablespoons vegetable or chicken bouillon

2 cups chopped Mexican squash

⅓ cup cilantro sprigs

lime slices for juice

1   Bring 8 cups water to a boil in a large saucepan over medium heat. Add cabbage, carrots, celery, and chayote. Simmer for 15 minutes.

2   While vegetables simmer, prepare tomato sauce mixture. Heat oil in a medium saucepan over medium-low heat. Add onion and garlic. Cook until tender, about 3 minutes. Stir in tomato sauce and bouillon. Boil for 5 minutes.

3   Combine vegetable and tomato sauce mixtures. Bring to a boil. Add Mexican squash and cilantro. Cover and cook for 5 minutes.

4   Serve with a sprinkle of lime juice.

CREMA DE CHAYOTE
Cream of Chayote Soup

Chayote is so popular in Mexico that it has made its way into the produce section of my local grocery store. Also known as chayote squash or pear-shaped squash, it is bright green and mild in flavor. It is cooked pretty much the same way you would cook zucchini. Cream of chayote soup is a great way to introduce someone to this funny-looking gourd, and I would consider it a kid-friendly recipe because of its mild flavor and smooth texture.

PREPARATION TIME: 10 MINUTES
COOK TIME: 35 MINUTES
SERVES 4

2 tablespoons salted butter

1 tablespoon olive oil

1 cup roughly chopped white onion

2 garlic cloves, roughly chopped

3 chayote squash, seeds removed, chopped (about 6 cups)

1 cup evaporated milk

2 teaspoons vegetable bouillon

fresh cracked black pepper to taste

dried or fresh chives for serving

croutons for serving

1   Heat butter and olive oil in a large sauté pan over medium heat. Add onion and garlic. Stir until onion becomes translucent, about 5 minutes.

2   Add chayote and cook for 20 minutes or until fork-tender. Remove from heat and let cool.

3   Transfer mixture to blender and blend until smooth. Return mixture to sauté pan over medium-low heat. Stir in evaporated milk and bouillon. Cook for 10 minutes, stirring frequently.

4   Season with black pepper and top with chives and croutons.

SOPA DE FIDEO
Fideo Soup

Fideo is the soup of my childhood and pretty much a weekly meal for us. Whether the noodles are in the form of stars, the alphabet, or seashells, this beloved dish is full of comfort, warmth, and nostalgia and will brighten anyone's day.

PREPARATION TIME: 15 MINUTES
COOK TIME: 20 MINUTES
SERVES 4

3 tablespoons canola oil

3.5 ounces dry fideo pasta

½ cup finely chopped white onion

1 garlic clove, finely chopped

4 ounces tomato sauce

1 teaspoon chicken or vegetable bouillon

¼ teaspoon black pepper

salt to taste

5 cilantro sprigs

TOPPINGS

chopped cilantro

chopped avocado

crumbled cotija cheese

lime juice

1   Heat oil in a large saucepan over medium-low heat. Add pasta. Stir until pasta darkens in color but does not burn.

2   Add onion and garlic. Stir until onion is translucent.

3   Stir in tomato sauce. Cook for 1 minute.

4   Add 6 cups hot water, bouillon, and black pepper. Partially cover and bring to a boil. Boil for 8–10 minutes. Season with salt if needed.

5   Remove from heat. Add cilantro sprigs. Cover and let stand for 15 minutes.

6   Discard cilantro sprigs. Serve. Garnish with chopped cilantro, avocado, cotija cheese, and a sprinkle of lime juice.

POZOLE ROJO DE JACA
Jackfruit Red Pozole

A big bowl of red pozole always meant happy moments and big celebrations in my family. In particular, during the party after a big wedding, called a *tornaboda*, the bride and groom's family and close friends gather, usually at the parents' home, to enjoy some spicy pozole. The "intimate" gathering usually consisted of a full house, loud with laughter, until the early hours of the morning or until the pozole ran out. Extra folding chairs would line the walls of the living room and kitchen. If you arrived early, you were lucky enough to claim a seat. The tornaboda was a great way to catch up with friends and relatives who traveled from afar to attend the wedding, and pozole was considered a cure for the awaiting hangover.

PREPARATION TIME: 35 MINUTES
COOK TIME: 60 MINUTES
SERVES 12–14

6 guajillo chiles, stems and seeds removed and skins wiped clean

4 ancho chiles, stems and seeds removed and skins wiped clean

½ cup roughly chopped onion

6 garlic cloves, roughly chopped

1 teaspoon oregano

1 teaspoon salt

1 tablespoon cooking oil

2 (14-ounce) cans young jackfruit, drained

3 teaspoons vegetable bouillon, divided

1 (25-ounce) can hominy, drained

2 dried bay leaves

TOPPINGS

sliced radishes

shredded cabbage

finely chopped onion

dried Mexican oregano

lime juice

1   Bring 6 cups water to a boil in a large saucepan. Remove from heat and add chile skins. Soak for 20 minutes or until skins are soft.

2   Transfer chile skins to blender. Add onion, garlic, oregano, salt, and 2 cups water. Blend until smooth. Run through a fine mesh strainer. Set aside.

3   Heat oil in a large pot over medium heat. Add jackfruit and season with 1 teaspoon bouillon. Stir, breaking pieces into smaller bite-sized pieces. Cook for 10 minutes.

4   Carefully pour in sauce. Cook for 20 minutes, stirring frequently.

5   Add 9 cups water, remaining 2 teaspoons bouillon, hominy, and bay leaves. Cover. Cook for 20 minutes.

6   Serve with radishes, cabbage, onion, oregano, and a sprinkle of lime juice.

LENTEJAS EN CALDO DE TOMATE

Lentils in Tomato Broth

A big *olla* of lentils on the stovetop always meant two things: spring was near and Lenten season was about to begin. I love my *sopa de lentejas* just as much as I love *sopa de fideo* (page 87). The meal is simple and humble, yet so full of flavor. Now I make it for my son the same way my mother made it for me. I'm delighted that he enjoys it just as much as I did.

PREPARATION TIME: 10 MINUTES
COOK TIME 35 MINUTES
SERVES 8

1 pound dry lentils, rinsed

4 Roma tomatoes, roughly chopped

⅓ cup roughly chopped white onion

2 garlic cloves

½ cup roughly chopped red bell pepper

3 tablespoons canola oil

1½ teaspoons vegetable bouillon

2 large carrots, finely chopped

1 fresh cilantro bunch

1 teaspoon salt

1 Bring 6 cups water to a boil in a large saucepan over medium heat. Reduce heat to medium-low and add lentils. Cook for 15 minutes.

2 While lentils cook, add tomatoes, onion, garlic, bell pepper, and 2 cups water to a blender. Blend until smooth.

3 Heat oil in large sauté pan over medium heat. Add blended tomato mixture and bouillon. Cook for 5 minutes, stirring frequently.

4 Add tomato mixture, carrots, cilantro bunch, and salt to lentils. Cook for 15 minutes or until lentils and carrots are tender.

GUISO DE COLIFLOR EN SALSA VERDE

Cauliflower Stew in Salsa Verde

This stew was created during a refrigerator cleanup. With leftover cauliflower florets, hominy, cooked cactus, and salsa verde, something magical happened that day in the kitchen. A bowl of this is perfect for a cold winter day or as a make-ahead dinner to freeze and enjoy later.

◇◇◇

PREPARATION TIME: 15 MINUTES
COOK TIME: 40 MINUTES
SERVES 8

4 cups (1 head) cauliflower florets

1 tablespoon cooking oil

2 medium Yukon Gold potatoes, peeled and cubed (2 cups)

2 cups salsa verde (page 34)

½ teaspoon sea salt

2 bay leaves

1 cup canned hominy, drained

1 cup cooked cactus (page 15)

cubed panela cheese for serving

sliced avocado for serving

cooked white rice for serving

1   Bring 6 cups water to a boil in a large saucepan over medium heat. Add cauliflower florets. Boil for 5 minutes. Immediately remove from heat and drain.

2   Heat oil in a large saucepan over medium heat. Add potatoes. Cook for 5 minutes, stirring frequently.

3   Add 2 cups water, salsa verde, salt, and bay leaves. Boil for 5 minutes.

4   Add cauliflower florets, hominy, and cactus. Cover and reduce heat to low. Simmer for 25 minutes.

5   Top with panela cheese and avocado and serve with white rice.

GUISO DE VERDOLAGAS CON PAPAS

Purslane and Potato Stew

My mom has a *verdolagas* (purslane) plant in a shaded little area at the rear of her house in Texas. If you walk by it, it looks just like weeds. Its leaves are abundant, and we consider it a little culinary treasure every time we take a generous handful to make this dish. Who knew this humble plant was so delicious and comforting when cooked as a stew? Purslane can be found in the produce section of the Latin grocery store early summer through late fall. It can be enjoyed fresh in salads as well.

PREPARATION TIME: 10 MINUTES
COOK TIME: 40 MINUTES
SERVES 6

2 bunches purslane, rinsed (about 4 packed cups)
1 large white onion, divided
2 garlic cloves
1 teaspoon salt, divided
1 tablespoon cooking oil
1 Roma tomato, chopped

2 large jalapeños, veins and seeds removed, sliced in strips
1½ cups peeled and cubed russet potato
⅓ cup chopped fresh cilantro
½ teaspoon black pepper
tortillas or tostadas for serving

1   Combine 2 cups water, purslane, ½ onion, garlic, and ½ teaspoon salt in a large saucepan. Cover and cook over medium heat for 12 minutes.

2   Discard onion and garlic cloves. Transfer purslane from saucepan into a large bowl. Do not throw away water purslane cooked in.

3   Roughly chop cooked purslane and place back in bowl. Chop remaining ½ onion.

4   Heat oil in a large sauté pan over medium heat. Add chopped onion, tomato, and jalapeño. Cook for 5 minutes.

5   Add potatoes. Cook for 10 minutes.

6   Add purslane and cilantro. Cook for 5 minutes, folding all ingredients together.

7   Return the saucepan with purslane water to stove burner. Heat over medium heat. Add all the contents of the sauté pan to the water. Stir. Cook for 5–7 minutes or until potatoes are tender. Season with pepper and remaining ½ teaspoon salt.

8   Serve with tortillas or tostadas.

SOPA DE MILPA

Garden Soup

This humble and beautiful soup is popular in central Mexico. It's made with vegetables typically harvested in a *milpa* (cornfield). The basic ingredients include zucchini squash, squash blossoms, corn, epazote, and poblano chiles in a light vegetable or chicken broth. Everyone has their own version; many add mushrooms, cactus, and green beans. It's a great soup to prepare when you have a few leftover vegetables.

PREPARATION TIME: 15 MINUTES
COOK TIME: 35 MINUTES
SERVES 8

2 roasted poblano chiles (page 12)

2 tablespoons olive oil

¾ cup chopped yellow onion

2 garlic cloves, chopped

2 cups chopped Mexican squash

2 cups white corn

8 cups vegetable broth

2 epazote leaves

2 cups squash blossoms

1 teaspoon salt or to taste

shredded Oaxaca cheese for garnish

1   Slice roasted poblano chiles in strips and set aside.

2   Heat oil in a large saucepan over medium heat. Add onion and garlic. Sauté for 2 minutes, stirring frequently.

3   Add poblano strips. Cook for 1 minute.

4   Add squash and corn. Cook for 5 minutes, stirring frequently.

5   Add broth and epazote. Decrease heat to medium-low. Cook for 15 minutes.

6   Add squash blossoms and season with salt. Bring to a simmer. Immediately remove from heat.

7   Serve. Top with Oaxaca cheese.

SOPA DE CHUALES
Spicy Chuales Soup

Chuales are pieces of cracked corn that are cooked and added to soups, stews, and salads. They are popular in Coahuila, where I am from, during the Lenten season. In the state of Chihuahua, they are known as *choales* or *chacales*.

Chuales soup was my favorite meal during Lent. The corn pieces were softened by the broth but still had a tender bite to them. Not only did I love eating this comforting soup, but I had fun preparing it in my grandmother's kitchen. As an eight-year-old, my duty was to clean and rinse the white pebbled corn in a big pot full of water—a job I took very seriously.

◇◇

PREPARATION TIME: 10 MINUTES
COOK TIME: 50 MINUTES
SERVES 10–12

6 dried guajillo chiles, stems and seeds removed and skins wiped clean

3 dried arbol chiles, stems and seeds removed and skins wiped clean

1 pound cracked white corn, rinsed and drained

6 garlic cloves, divided

2 dried bay leaves

1 teaspoon dried oregano

½ teaspoon ground cumin

2½ teaspoons salt, divided

2 tablespoons corn oil

1 cup chopped white onion

1 large Roma tomato, chopped

½ cup chopped fresh cilantro sprigs

lime wedges for serving

1   Place chiles in a medium saucepan with enough water to cover. Bring to a rapid boil over medium heat. Boil for 1 minute. Remove from heat and set aside. Do not throw away water.

2   Place cracked corn in a medium saucepan with enough water to cover. Heat over medium-low heat for 10 minutes until al dente. Remove from heat and drain.

3   While cracked corn cooks, prepare chile sauce. Place 3 garlic cloves, bay leaves, oregano, cumin, ½ teaspoon salt, softened chiles, and 3 cups chile water in a blender. Blend until smooth. Run through a strainer. Set aside. Finely chop remaining garlic cloves.

4   Heat oil in a large saucepan over medium heat. Add onion. Cook for 2 minutes or until tender.

5   Add chopped garlic, tomato, and cilantro. Stir until tomatoes soften, about 4 minutes.

6   Add cracked corn. Stir for 2 minutes.

7   Add 8 cups water, chile sauce, and remaining 2 teaspoons salt. Cook for 30 minutes or until corn is soft.

8   Serve with lime wedges.

SOPA CREMOSA DE AGUACATE

Creamy Avocado Soup

I call this avocado cream soup "*mi sopa rápida*" ("my quick soup"). It's warm and comforting and makes a great satisfying lunch. Because avocado browns quickly when heated too long, the avocado is added during the last five minutes of preparation. As soon as it's ready, enjoy topped with crispy tortilla strips and some queso fresco. It's like a warm hug in a bowl.

PREPARATION TIME: 10 MINUTES
COOK TIME: 20 MINUTES
SERVES 4

¾ cup vegetable oil

6 corn tortillas, cut in thin strips

2 cups chopped avocado
  (about 1½ large avocados)

1 large jalapeño, seeds and veins removed

6 cups vegetable or chicken broth, divided

1 teaspoon vegetable or chicken bouillon

crumbled queso fresco for serving

1   Heat oil in a large pan over medium heat. Fry tortilla strips a handful at a time, about 3 minutes per batch. Transfer to a paper towel–lined plate. Set aside.

2   Combine avocado, jalapeño, and 1 cup broth in a blender. Blend until smooth. Set aside.

3   Heat remaining 5 cups broth in a large saucepan over medium heat. Bring to a boil, then reduce heat to medium-low.

4   Add avocado mixture and bouillon. Heat for 5 minutes, stirring constantly, making sure mixture becomes creamy with no lumps.

5   Serve immediately. Top with fried tortilla strips and crumbled queso fresco.

POZOLE VERDE CON CHAMPIÑONES

Green Pozole with Mushrooms

I love adding a little more spice to my pozole. Every time I'm boiling tomatillos for this dish, I like to throw in a couple of serrano chiles. The tanginess of cooked tomatillos, the spicy-sweet taste of poblanos, and the added lemon juice make an exquisite green broth. The meaty mushrooms and a mixture of crunchy radishes and crisp iceberg lettuce make it a complete hardy meal. Leftovers from this large batch can be frozen for up to three weeks.

PREPARATION TIME: 25 MINUTES
COOK TIME: 55 MINUTES
SERVES 10–12

8 medium tomatillos, husked and rinsed

2 serrano chiles, stems removed

3 jalapeños, stems removed

1 cup raw pepitas

3 poblano chiles, roasted, seeds and veins removed (page 12)

½ white onion

4 garlic cloves

2 large iceberg lettuce leaves

1 cup (packed) fresh cilantro sprigs

4 basil leaves

½ cup baby spinach

⅓ cup radish leaves

3 fresh oregano sprigs

2 tablespoons cooking oil

2½ tablespoons salt

1 (110-ounce) can hominy, drained and rinsed

7 cups (about 900 grams) shiitake mushrooms or any other brown mushroom, sliced

4 cups (about 236 grams) oyster mushrooms, torn

TOPPINGS

radish slices

finely diced white onion

chopped cilantro

shredded iceberg lettuce

crushed dried oregano

lime juice

1   Place tomatillos, serranos, and jalapeños in a medium saucepan with enough water to cover. Bring to a boil over medium-high heat. Boil about 15 minutes. Drain.

2   While tomatillos and chiles cook, heat pepitas on a medium skillet over medium-low heat. Stir frequently until they turn golden brown, about 7 minutes.

3   Combine tomatillos, all three chiles, pepitas, onion, and garlic cloves in a blender. Blend until smooth.

4   Add lettuce, cilantro, basil, baby spinach, radish leaves, oregano sprigs, and 1½ cups water. Blend until smooth.

5   Heat oil in a sauté pan over medium heat. Stir in blended mixture. Add salt. Bring to a boil. Cook 10 minutes, stirring frequently.

6   Place 6 liters (about 1.5 gallons) water in a large pot. Bring to a boil over medium heat. Add hominy. Boil for 20 minutes.

7   Add mushrooms and cooked green blended mixture. Stir, then cover. Bring to a boil and cook until mushrooms are tender, about 10 minutes.

8   Serve. Top with radish slices, onion, cilantro, lettuce, oregano, and a squeeze of lime juice.

SOPA DE QUESO CON PAPA Y RAJAS

Cheese Soup with Potato and Chile Strips

If I have to pick a soup that reminds me of home, this cheese soup with potato and chile strips has to be it. Brothy yet creamy, loaded with warm, softened queso fresco cubes, with a bit of green chile spice and starchy potatoes for texture, this is a complete meal all on its own. Serve it when you need comfort or to keep warm on a cold winter day.

PREPARATION TIME: 20 MINUTES
COOK TIME: 25 MINUTES
SERVES 6

2 tablespoons vegetable oil

¾ cup roughly chopped white onion

2 garlic cloves, finely chopped

2 cups chopped Roma tomato

4 cups peeled and chopped russet potato

¼ teaspoon oregano

¼ teaspoon black pepper

1 fresh cilantro bunch

1 tablespoon vegetable bouillon

1 cup milk, room temperature

2 poblano chiles, roasted and sliced in strips (page 12)

2 Anaheim chiles, roasted and sliced in strips

1½ cups queso fresco, cubed

1   Heat oil in a large pot over medium heat. Add onion and garlic. Cook for 5 minutes.

2   Add tomato. Cook for 5 minutes, stirring frequently.

3   Add 2 cups water, potato, oregano, black pepper, cilantro, and bouillon. Bring to a boil. Boil for 10 minutes.

4   Add milk and chile strips. Boil for 5 minutes.

5   Remove cilantro springs and discard. Turn heat off. Add cheese cubes. Cover pot to soften cheese. Serve.

SOPA AZTECA
Tortilla Soup

The first time I had sopa Azteca was in a beautiful restaurant in Oaxaca called La Olla. The restaurant is located next to Las Bugambilias, the bed and breakfast we stayed at, both owned by the Cabrera family.

The soup was not served typically; I had to assemble it. I was given a shallow bowl filled with thin tortilla strips accompanied by three other small bowls of cubed cheese, fried pasilla chile strips, and cubed avocado. Next to those small bowls was a tin pitcher filled with the warm silky-smooth soup. I poured the soup over the tortilla strips, added toppings, and enjoyed immediately so as to not lose the crunchiness of the delicate tortilla strips. I added *caldo* (broth) and toppings until they were gone.

It's been years since I've been back. But that soup flavor and the serving process is one of my fondest memories. Now, every time I make my version of sopa Azteca, I serve it the same way I was served years ago.

PREPARATION TIME: 20 MINUTES
COOK TIME: 50 MINUTES
SERVES 8

1 ancho chile, stems and seeds removed

3 pasilla chiles, stems and seeds removed, divided

¾ cup plus 1 tablespoon vegetable oil, divided

10 corn tortillas, sliced in thin strips

10 Roma tomatoes, halved

½ medium white onion, roughly chopped

3 large garlic cloves

1 tablespoon chicken or vegetable bouillon

6 cups low-sodium chicken or vegetable broth

1 fresh epazote bunch (about 10 sprigs)

TOPPINGS

cubed panela cheese

cubed avocado

Mexican crema or crème fraîche

1   Bring 3 cups water to a boil in a medium saucepan over medium heat. Add ancho chile and 2 pasilla chiles. Boil for 2 minutes. Remove from heat and let chiles hydrate for 15 minutes. Do not throw away water.

2   Slice the remaining pasilla chile into thin strips. Set aside.

3   Heat ¾ cup oil in a large frying pan over medium heat. Fry tortilla strips until golden brown. Transfer to a paper towel–lined plate to drain. Set aside.

4   Fry pasilla chile strips in the same oil for 20 seconds. Immediately transfer to a separate paper towel–lined plate to drain. Set aside.

5   Combine tomatoes, onion, garlic, hydrated chiles, and 1 cup chile water in blender. Blend until smooth. Run through a strainer and set aside.

6   Heat remaining tablespoon oil in a large saucepan over medium-low heat. Add chile sauce and stir in bouillon. Cook for 10 minutes.

7   Add broth and epazote. Simmer for 25 minutes. Remove epazote sprigs and discard.

8   To serve, place a handful of fried tortilla strips in a soup bowl. Ladle soup in bowl. Top with cheese, avocado, crema, and fried pasilla chile strips.

CALDO DE POLLO
Mexican Chicken Soup

Caldo de pollo comes together with any vegetables you have in your refrigerator. Sometimes I add cabbage, and sometimes I add chayote if squash is not available. No matter your veggie combination, the chicken broth, aromatic cilantro, and mint keep this caldo flavorful. Serve it with some Mexican rice, warm tortillas, and a squeeze of lime juice for the full experience.

PREPARATION TIME: 10 MINUTES
COOK TIME: 45 MINUTES
SERVES 8–10

1½ pounds bone-in chicken
   (combination of legs, wings, or thighs)

½ white onion

4 garlic cloves

2 celery stalks, chopped in large pieces

½ teaspoon chicken bouillon or salt

2 corn cobs, sliced in 8–10 rounds

2 medium carrots, sliced

2 large gold potatoes, chopped in large pieces

6 cilantro sprigs

4 mint sprigs

2 Mexican squash, sliced

lime juice for serving

Mexican rice for serving (page 125)

1   Bring 12 cups water to a boil in a large pot over medium heat. While water heats, remove any fatty chicken pieces.

2   Add chicken, onion, garlic, celery, and bouillon (or salt) to pot. Decrease heat to medium-low. Boil for 15 minutes. Remove any foamy water that rises to the top with a large spoon and discard.

3   Add corn, carrots, potatoes, cilantro, and mint. Cook for 20 minutes or until potato pieces are tender.

4   Add squash and turn off heat. Let squash cook for 10 minutes.

5   Serve. Sprinkle with lime juice and add one or two spoonfuls of Mexican rice.

Guarniciones
(Sides)

CALABACITAS MEXICANAS
Mexican-Style Squash

Calabacitas (little squash) is a term of endearment for this beloved side dish. It was the only vegetable dish I truly loved as a child (and still do as an adult). Made with Mexican squash, onion, corn, and asadero cheese, this dish is guaranteed to be a kid favorite. I've amped up this version with the addition of tomatoes and some serrano chile heat (which are completely optional). I've also switched up the cheese to a drier sprinkle of cotija. Serve this dish with a stack of corn or flour tortillas, and if the serranos are too hot, tame them with a dollop of sour cream.

PREPARATION TIME: 10 MINUTES
COOK TIME: 30 MINUTES
SERVES 4–6

2 tablespoons olive oil

½ cup chopped onion

3 garlic cloves, finely chopped

3 Roma tomatoes, chopped

1 serrano chile, veins and seeds removed, finely chopped (optional)

1 teaspoon salt, divided

3 Mexican squash, chopped (2½ cups)

1 cup corn

⅓ cup chopped fresh cilantro

crumbled cotija cheese for serving

sour cream for serving

1   Heat oil in a large skillet over medium heat. Add onion. Cook for 4 minutes or until translucent. Add garlic and cook for 1 minute, stirring frequently.

2   Add tomatoes, serrano chile (optional), and ½ teaspoon salt. Cook for 5 minutes, stirring frequently.

3   Add remaining ½ teaspoon salt, squash, corn, and cilantro. Stir to combine. Reduce heat to medium-low and cover. Cook for 20 minutes.

4   Remove from heat. Serve with cotija cheese and sour cream.

SOPA DE RELIQUIA
Reliquia Pasta

In Torreón, where I am from, many people attend reliquias. A *reliquia* is a religious event organized by a family or a group of families in which they make an offering to a saint or the Virgin of Guadalupe. The offering is an annual celebration that includes a feast and prayer. Sometimes *matachines* (dancers) or a band are hired to perform and announce the start of the event. After praying has concluded, a meal is served.

Whether one attended the prayer or not, anyone in the community is welcome to bring their own plate for the food to be served on and enjoyed at home. It's customary to serve spicy red chile pork stew and seven pasta dishes (*sopas secas*). The pasta can be elbow macaroni, alphabet, stars, fideo, ziti, spaghetti, or shells.

PREPARATION TIME: 10 MINUTES
COOK TIME: 40 MINUTES
SERVES 6–8

1 pound ziti pasta or any other pasta (your choice)

4 large Roma tomatoes

¾ cup roughly chopped white onion

1 large clove garlic

3 tablespoons canola oil

¼ teaspoon black pepper

1 tablespoon chicken or vegetable bouillon

chopped fresh cilantro for garnish

crumbled queso fresco for garnish

1   Cook pasta according to package directions. Drain and set aside.

2   Place tomatoes in a large saucepan and add enough water to cover. Bring to a boil over medium heat. Boil for 10 minutes or until tomato skins begin to peel. Drain.

3   Combine tomatoes, onion, garlic, and 1 cup water in a blender. Blend until smooth.

4   Heat oil in a large saucepan. Stir in sauce, black pepper, and bouillon. Boil for 10 minutes.

5   Add cooked pasta. Decrease heat to medium-low. Cook for 10 minutes, stirring frequently.

6   Serve. Garnish with cilantro and queso fresco.

NOPALES EN CHILE COLORADO

Cactus in Red Chile Sauce

If you haven't already noticed, there are a few recipes in this book that include cooked cactus. *Nopales* have always been a big part of my life. I grew up chopping tender pads off the cactus grown on our patio. I learned how to remove thorns and chop and cook the pads. Because I loved them so much, my mom would tell me "*Tú nunca te vas a morir de hambre.*" ("You will never die of hunger.") Whether in a salad, a taco, a smoothie, or a stew, I've always loved their taste. During *Lenten* (season of Lent), cactus in red chile sauce was always part of our meatless Fridays. I like to serve it with rice (page 125) and a big stack of freshly made corn tortillas (page 19).

PREPARATION TIME: 20 MINUTES
COOK TIME: 25 MINUTES
SERVES 6

5 dried guajillo chiles	1 tablespoon canola oil
3 dried ancho chiles	½ cup sliced white onion
2 garlic cloves	3 cups chopped cooked cactus (page 15)
3 whole cloves	1½ teaspoons salt
1 teaspoon dried oregano	10 fresh cilantro sprigs

1   Rinse chiles and pat dry with paper towel. Cut stems with kitchen scissors. Do not remove seeds.

2   Place chiles in a medium saucepan and add enough water to cover. Bring to a boil over medium heat. Boil for 5 minutes. Use a large spoon to press down on the chiles to keep them from floating to the top. Remove from heat and let them continue to soak in hot water for 10 minutes.

3   Do not throw away water. Transfer soaked chiles to a blender. Add 1 cup chile water, garlic, cloves, and oregano to blender. Blend until smooth.

4   Heat oil in a large sauté pan over medium heat. Add onion and cook until translucent, about 2 minutes. Add cactus and cook for 2 more minutes.

5   Run sauce through a strainer into sauté pan. Stir. Add 3 cups water and salt. Bring to a boil. Add cilantro sprigs and reduce heat. Cook for 12 minutes.

6   Serve.

RAJAS POBLANAS CON CREMA

Creamy Poblano Chile Strips

In our home, the crackling sound of poblano skins over an open flame and the smoky spicy aroma could mean only one thing: rajas con crema were cooking.

Poblanos are great stuffed and battered, but have you ever had roasted poblano strips with cheese, cream, and corn? Absolute heaven. Everyone has their own version of how to enjoy rajas con crema. I like mine with extra cheese and wrapped in a warm corn tortilla.

PREPARATION TIME: 15 MINUTES
COOK TIME: 25 MINUTES
SERVES 6

2 large poblano chiles, roasted (page 12)
2 tablespoons cooking oil
½ cup sliced white onion
2 garlic cloves, finely chopped

1 cup white corn
¾ cup Mexican cream or crème fraîche
½ cup queso fresco, cubed
corn tortillas for serving

1   Slice roasted poblano chiles in strips. Set aside.

2   Heat oil in a large sauté pan over medium heat. Add onion and garlic. Cook until translucent, about 3 minutes.

3   Add poblano strips and corn. Cook for 12 minutes, stirring frequently.

4   Decrease heat to low and stir in cream. Season with salt and pepper. Simmer for 5 minutes.

5   Add cheese. Cover and remove from heat. Let cheese soften for 5–10 minutes.

6   Serve with warm corn tortillas.

FRIJOLES DE LA OLLA

Beans from the Pot

In my freezer, you are sure to find a few storage containers filled with frozen frijoles de la olla. I make a large batch to always have ready for enfrijoladas (page 48) or frijoles maneados (page 122) and to, of course, make refried beans with. Just fry them with a little garlic oil and mash them with a bean or potato masher.

PREPARATION TIME: 10 MINUTES
COOK TIME: 2 HOURS
MAKES 12 CUPS

4 cups dry pinto or Peruano beans

1 medium white onion, sliced in half

3 large garlic cloves

1 tablespoon olive oil

1 tablespoon salt or to taste

1   In a large pot, bring 12 cups water to a boil over medium-high heat.

2   While the water comes to a boil, clean beans of any pebbles and debris. Rinse and drain beans.

3   Add beans, both onion halves, garlic, and oil to boiling water. Reduce heat to medium-low and cover. Cook for 1 hour 45 minutes. Check beans every 20 minutes. Stir and watch for water to begin to evaporate. When water level drops, add boiling water to keep beans from drying out while they cook.

4   After 1 hour 45 minutes, add salt to your preference. Stir and continue cooking for 15 minutes more or until beans are tender. Add more salt if needed.

5   Discard onion and garlic. If storing, allow beans to cool completely before refrigerating or freezing.

FRIJOLES MANEADOS

Stirred Beans

Frijoles maneados is a bean dip like no other. The name *maneados*, meaning "stirred," comes from the special dried guajillo and arbol chile sauce stirred in through the entire cooking process, melding the spicy and smoky flavors together. Shredded manchego cheese gives this dip a gooey, easy-to-scoop consistency.

PREPARATION TIME: 15 MINUTES
COOK TIME: 20 MINUTES
SERVES 16

4 dried guajillo chiles, stems and seeds removed and skins wiped clean

1 dried arbol chile, stem and seeds removed and skin wiped clean

½ cup roughly chopped white onion

3 garlic cloves

¼ teaspoon ground cumin

1 teaspoon salt or to taste

⅓ cup cooking oil

3 tablespoons butter

5 cups cooked Peruano or pinto beans, drained

2 cups grated manchego cheese

tortilla chips for serving

1   Bring 4 cups water to a boil in a medium saucepan over medium heat. Remove from heat, add dried chiles, and set aside to soak for 10 minutes. Do not throw away water.

2   Add hydrated chiles, 1 cup chile water, onion, garlic, cumin, and salt to a blender. Blend until smooth.

3   Heat oil and butter in a large skillet over medium heat. When butter has melted, add blended chile mixture and stir. Increase heat to medium-high and cook for 5 minutes, stirring frequently.

4   Decrease heat back to medium. Stir in beans and mash with bean or potato masher until a paste forms, about 10 minutes.

5   Add grated cheese and stir until cheese melts. Taste test to check if additional salt is needed. Remove from heat.

6   Transfer to a large serving bowl and serve with tortilla chips.

ARROZ MEXICANO

Mexican Rice

One very important tip my mom gave me when making Mexican rice is to include ripe, bright red Roma tomatoes. I like to set out the tomatoes on the kitchen counter a couple of days beforehand to intensify their color and flavor. No canned tomato sauce is needed.

¼ white onion

2 large garlic cloves

2 ripe Roma tomatoes

2 tablespoons cooking oil

1 cup long-grain rice

2 cups vegetable or chicken broth

½ teaspoon salt or to taste

chopped fresh cilantro for garnish (optional)

1   Place onion, garlic, and tomatoes in a blender. Blend until smooth.

2   Heat oil in a large sauté pan over medium heat. Add rice and fry, stirring frequently, until rice begins to brown, about 5 minutes.

3   Add tomato mixture and stir. Cook for 3 minutes.

4   Add broth and salt and stir. Bring to a boil. Decrease heat to low and cover. Cook for 20 minutes or until liquid has been absorbed by rice.

5   Garnish with cilantro. Fluff with fork and serve.

Platos Fuertes (Mains)

GORDITAS DE REQUESÓN Y ESPINACAS

Requesón and Spinach Gorditas

I love corn masa gorditas (corn flour pockets similar to pita bread) with requesón cheese. I make this version of requesón filling with spinach, and I like to assemble the gorditas a bit differently. I prefer an almost tortilla-thin pocket. Because these are thinner than traditional gorditas, stuffing them before cooking is easier and less messy. You can make these the traditional way too; just make sure the gordita is thicker when cooking, then slice and stuff with filling.

If you are unable to find requesón, ricotta cheese works just as well. Requesón can be found at any Latin supermarket. It is usually sold by weight in the deli or prepared food section.

PREPARATION TIME: 30 MINUTES
COOK TIME: 50 MINUTES
MAKES 12

4 cups masa harina (corn flour)	1 teaspoon vegetable bouillon
½ teaspoon salt	5 ounces baby spinach, chopped
2 tablespoons corn oil	2 cups requesón or ricotta cheese
2 Roma tomatoes, finely chopped	roasted serrano chiles for serving
½ white onion, finely chopped (about 1 cup)	habanero-spiced pickled onions for serving (page 30)
2 large garlic cloves, chopped	salsa for serving

1 Combine masa harina, salt, and 3 cups hot water in a large bowl. Mix with a large spoon until cool enough to touch, then knead until dough is smooth and does not stick to hands. If dough is too dry, add more water 1 tablespoon at a time. Cover with a kitchen towel and set aside for 15 minutes.

2 Heat oil in a large sauté pan over medium heat. Add tomatoes and onion. Cook for 3 minutes, stirring rapidly.

3 Add garlic and bouillon. Cook for 5 minutes until mixture begins to release liquid.

4 Add spinach. Cook for 2 minutes or until spinach wilts. Remove from heat. Tilt pan over sink to drain liquid, using a spoon or spatula to press mixture against the pan to squeeze out any excess. Transfer mixture to a bowl. Add requesón and stir to mix thoroughly.

5 Brush a bit of oil on a skillet or comal and heat over medium heat.

6 Divide dough into 24 golf ball–sized pieces. Roll each piece between the palms of your hands. If dough is too dry, wet hands. Place dough ball between two thick plastic sheets. Press with hands (or plate) into a 3-inch disc. Set aside and repeat with remaining balls.

7 Spoon 2 tablespoons mixture onto the middle of a disc. Cover with second disc (sandwiching filling between discs), and pinch edges with fingers to seal. Place on hot skillet for 5–7 minutes on each side or until dough has cooked thoroughly. Transfer to serving tray. Cover with a kitchen towel or plastic wrap to keep gorditas from drying. Repeat with remaining dough and mixture.

8 Slice gorditas open. Add roasted serrano chiles, pickled onions, or your favorite salsa.

TETELAS DE FRIJOLES NEGROS

Black Bean Tetelas

During my traveling through Oaxaca, I discovered tetelas de frijol. *Tetelas* are triangular masa pockets stuffed with a thick, savory filling. They can be topped with salsa, cream, or crumbled cheese. Black refried beans are the perfect filling because they are easy to spread and stay in place during the cooking process. To make tetelas, you'll need a tortilla press, a comal (griddle), and two sheets of plastic; you can use a gallon-sized plastic freezer bag cut in half for the plastic.

◇◇

PREPARATION TIME: 30 MINUTES
COOK TIME: 40 MINUTES
MAKES 12

2 tablespoons cooking oil

½ cup chopped white onion

1 (15-ounce) can no salt added black beans, drained

1 teaspoon garlic salt

2 cups blue or regular masa harina (corn flour)

1½ cups warm water

TOPPINGS

Mexican crema or crème fraîche

crumbled cotija cheese

salsa

pico de gallo

1   Heat oil in a medium saucepan over medium heat. Add onion and cook for 2 minutes or until translucent.

2   Add beans. Bring to a boil and mash using a potato or bean masher. Reduce heat.

3   Add garlic salt. Simmer for 8 minutes, stirring frequently. Remove from heat and let cool.

4   Preheat griddle, skillet, or comal over medium heat.

5   Combine masa harina and water in a large bowl. Mix with hands until a wet paste forms. Mixture should be pliable. Add more water by the tablespoon if needed. Set aside for 15 minutes.

6   Divide dough into 12 balls. Place in a bowl and cover with a kitchen towel while working to avoid drying out.

7   Line a tortilla press with two large plastic sheets. Place masa ball in between sheets and gently press into a 4-inch disc.

8   Remove top plastic sheet and spread 2 tablespoons of bean mixture in the center of the masa disc. Using the plastic sheet under the masa disc, fold over one side of the disc, toward the center, so it covers part of the filling. Repeat twice more so the dough resembles a triangle.

9   Transfer masa triangle to hot griddle, seams down. Cook for 3 minutes. Flip and cook for 5 minutes. Flip again and cook until dark spots appear, about 2 minutes. Transfer to a platter and cover with cloth napkin to keep warm. Repeat with remaining ingredients.

10 Serve warm topped with Mexican crema, cotija cheese, salsa, or pico de gallo.

TACOS DE NOPALES CON CHORIZO DE SOYA

Cactus and Soy Chorizo Tacos

When I cook a big batch of nopales, I reserve some to cook with my scrambled eggs, some to add to soups, and some to prepare these tacos with. These tacos burst with flavor. The nopales are cooked with thick onion strips and soy chorizo. You can also use pork or beef chorizo if you prefer. Want to add a little spice? Top your tacos with big dollops of salsa verde (page 34).

PREPARATION TIME: 10 MINUTES
COOK TIME: 45 MINUTES
MAKES 10

½ cup cooking oil, divided

½ white onion, chopped in strips

1 (11-ounce) package soy chorizo

3 cups chopped cooked cactus (page 15)

10 corn tortillas

salsa verde for serving

sour cream for serving

1   Heat 3 tablespoons oil in a large sauté pan over medium-low heat. Add onion and stir until soft, about 3 minutes.

2   Add soy chorizo. Cook about 10 minutes, breaking up chorizo with a large spoon.

3   Stir in cactus. Cook for 10 minutes or until all ingredients have mixed well together. Remove from heat and set aside.

4   Heat remaining ⅓ cup oil in medium frying pan over medium heat. Place corn tortilla in hot oil and fry for 30 seconds. Flip with large spatula. Add ⅓ cup soy chorizo and cactus mixture to tortilla and fold tortilla in half. Fry until golden brown, about 1 minute on each side. Transfer to a paper towel–lined plate. Repeat with remaining tortillas and mixture.

5   Serve with salsa verde and sour cream.

TINGA DE ZANAHORIA Y FLOR DE JAMAICA

Carrot and Hibiscus Tinga

Traditionally, *tinga* is a shredded chicken or beef stew dry enough to be scooped with tostadas or corn tortillas. This meatless version is just as phenomenal. I find that the sweetness of sautéed carrots and the tanginess of hibiscus blooms pair really well. Adding canned smoky chipotles in adobo gives this colorful dish a spicy punch.

PREPARATION TIME 15 MINUTES
COOK TIME 35 MINUTES
SERVES 6

2 cups dried hibiscus flower blooms, rinsed and drained

4 Roma tomatoes, roughly chopped

4 chipotle peppers in adobo sauce

2 teaspoons vegetable or chicken bouillon

2 tablespoons vegetable oil

1 cup sliced white onion

2 bay leaves

4 cups shredded or spiralized carrots (about 6 carrots)

warm corn tortillas for serving

1   Combine hibiscus and 4 cups water in a large saucepan over medium heat. Simmer for 10 minutes or until blooms are tender. Remove from heat, set aside, and let cool. Drain.

2   Place tomatoes, chipotle peppers, and bouillon in a blender. Blend until smooth. Run through a strainer. Set aside.

3   Heat oil in a large sauté pan over medium heat. Add onion and cook until tender, about 3 minutes.

4   Add tomato mixture and bay leaves. Bring to a simmer. Cover and cook for 10 minutes.

5   Add shredded carrots and hibiscus blooms. Cook for 10 minutes, stirring frequently.

6   Remove bay leaves. Serve with warm corn tortillas.

ENCHILADAS POBLANAS DE ZANAHORIA Y CHAMPIÑONES

Carrot and Mushroom Enchiladas Poblanas

This earthy, smoky poblano chile cream sauce is very versatile. It's great on baked fish and grilled shrimp, but I like it best enveloping warm corn tortillas stuffed with meaty mushrooms and perfectly seasoned cooked carrots. Make plenty. Your family will love this rich and creamy savory meal.

PREPARATION TIME: 30 MINUTES
COOK TIME: 20 MINUTES
SERVES 4–6

SAUCE

6 medium poblano chiles, roasted (page 12)

1 cup evaporated milk

½ cup sour cream

1 teaspoon chicken or vegetable bouillon

FILLING

2 tablespoons corn oil

½ yellow onion, finely chopped (about ¾ cup)

2 large garlic cloves, chopped

2 large carrots, finely chopped (about 1¼ cups)

10 ounces brown or white button mushrooms, chopped

1 teaspoon vegetable bouillon

OTHER

¼ cup butter

10–12 corn tortillas, warmed

½ cup sliced red onion for serving

crumbled cotija cheese for serving

1   Cut chiles open and remove seeds and veins. Place chiles in a blender. Add evaporated milk, sour cream, and bouillon. Blend until smooth. Set aside.

2   Next, prepare filling. Heat oil in a large sauté pan over medium heat. Add onion and garlic. Cook for 2 minutes, stirring frequently. Add carrots. Cook for 5 minutes, stirring frequently. Add mushrooms and bouillon. Cook for 10 minutes or until mushrooms are tender and carrots are cooked through. Set aside and keep warm.

3   Melt butter in a large saucepan over medium-low heat. Pour in poblano sauce. Stir and bring to a boil. Boil for 30 seconds (not minutes). Remove from heat and set aside.

4   Place 2–3 tablespoons filling mixture in a corn tortilla. Roll and arrange on a large plate or in a shallow casserole dish. Repeat with remaining tortillas and filling.

5   Pour warm poblano sauce over stuffed tortillas. Top with red onion and a sprinkle of cotija cheese. Serve.

ENCHILADAS ROJAS CON CALABACITA

Red Enchiladas with Mexican Squash

Enchiladas don't have to be just cheese, salsa, and tortilla; they can also be the perfect way to incorporate vegetables in your meals. These red enchiladas with Mexican squash make a complete meal everyone will be excited to enjoy. I like to serve them with rice (page 125) and a tall glass of mango agua fresca (page 175).

PREPARATION TIME: 25 MINUTES
COOKING TIME: 50 MINUTES
MAKES 12

SAUCE

10 dried guajillo chiles, veins and seeds removed

2 dried ancho chiles, veins and seeds removed

2 cups vegetable or chicken broth

3 garlic cloves, roughly chopped

¼ teaspoon dried Mexican oregano

⅛ teaspoon whole cumin

1 teaspoon salt

1 tablespoon cooking oil

TOPPING

½ tablespoon cooking oil

1 cup finely chopped white onion

4 cups finely chopped Mexican squash

1 teaspoon salt

½ teaspoon ground black pepper

2 Roma tomatoes, chopped

OTHER

⅓ cup cooking oil

12 corn tortillas

2 cups crumbled panela cheese

¼ cup finely chopped white onion

cotija cheese for topping

1   Place dried chiles in a large saucepan with enough water to cover. Bring to a boil. Cook for 2 minutes, then turn heat off. Let chiles hydrate in hot water for 10 minutes.

2   Transfer chiles to a blender. Add broth, garlic cloves, oregano, cumin, and salt. Blend until smooth. Run mixture through a strainer into a large bowl.

3   Heat 1 tablespoon oil in a large sauté pan. Add sauce and cover. Cook over low heat for 20 minutes.

4   While sauce cooks, make topping. Heat ½ tablespoon oil in a large frying pan. Add onion. Cook for 3 minutes. Add squash. Season with salt and pepper. Cook for 5 minutes. Add tomatoes. Cook for 10 minutes, stirring frequently. Remove from heat and set aside.

5   Heat ⅓ cup oil in a large frying pan. Fry each tortilla quickly, about 10 seconds on each side. Transfer to a paper towel–lined plate.

6   To assemble, dip each tortilla in enchilada sauce, covering both sides. Place on a plate and fill with 2–3 tablespoons panela cheese and ½ tablespoon onion. Fold in half and place on a serving platter. Repeat with remaining ingredients.

7   Top enchiladas with squash and tomato topping. Sprinkle with cotija cheese and serve.

Garlic Aioli

½ cup mayonnaise

3 large garlic
cloves, minced

1 ½ tablespoons
lime juice

1 tablespoon extra
virgin olive oil

1   Whisk together all ingredients in a medium bowl.
     Cover and refrigerate until ready to serve.

TACOS DE SALMÓN CON PICO DE GALLO DE PEPINO Y AIOLI DE AJO

Salmon Tacos with Cucumber Pico de Gallo and Garlic Aioli

Whenever we have a craving for fish, salmon is my go-to because it cooks so quickly and has a mild flavor. This recipe is so versatile because it can go from easy weeknight meal to a weekend taco party. The garlic aioli gives these tacos a tangy and zesty kick, while the cucumber pico de gallo gives them that spicy-fresh flavor no taco should be without.

PREPARATION TIME: 15 MINUTES
COOKING TIME: 20 MINUTES
MAKES 12

Cucumber Pico de Gallo

1 Roma tomato, finely chopped
1 cup finely chopped cucumber
¾ cup finely chopped red onion

1 large jalapeño, finely chopped
1 tablespoon lime juice
½ teaspoon salt or to taste

1   Toss together all ingredients in a medium bowl. Cover and refrigerate until ready to serve.

Salmon Tacos

1 teaspoon garlic salt
1½ teaspoons paprika
1 teaspoon chili powder
½ teaspoon ground cumin
½ teaspoon black ground pepper

1 teaspoon dried oregano, crushed
1 pound (about 4) salmon fillets with skin
2 tablespoons cooking oil
12 corn tortillas, warmed

TOPPINGS

shredded purple cabbage
chopped cilantro
lime juice

1   Combine garlic salt, paprika, chili powder, cumin, pepper, and oregano in a small bowl. Stir to mix well.

2   Dry salmon fillets with paper towels. Rub seasoning mixture on the flesh side.

3   Heat oil in a large pan over medium heat. Panfry salmon fillets flesh side down for 4 minutes. Flip to skin side and fry for 3–5 minutes. Remove from heat, pull off skin, and break salmon apart into small chunks.

4   To assemble, divide salmon between corn tortillas. Top with garlic aioli, cucumber pico de gallo, purple cabbage, cilantro, and a squeeze of lime juice.

CHILES RELLENOS EN SALSA DE TOMATE

Stuffed Poblano Chiles on Tomato Sauce

Chile relleno days involve everyone in my family. Stuffed chiles are not as labor-intensive as tamales, but they do create the same excitement in the kitchen. When my mom made chiles rellenos, she set aside some egg batter to make a kid-friendly version; instead of a spicy poblano chile, she used a corn tortilla, floured and battered in the same manner. Now I do the same for my son using this same recipe. Don't forget the tomato sauce! I consider it the star of the meal.

PREPARATION TIME: 30 MINUTES
COOK TIME: 30 MINUTES
SERVES 4

Stuffed Poblano Chiles

4 poblano chiles, roasted (page 12)	I cup canola oil
3½ cups shredded Oaxaca cheese	I cup all-purpose flour
½ small white onion, sliced in strips	sliced red onion for garnish
4 eggs	fresh oregano leaves for garnish
½ teaspoon salt	crumbled cotija cheese for garnish

1   Make a vertical slit with a small knife about half an inch from the bottom tip of each chile to half an inch from the stem. Using a small spoon, carefully scrape and scoop out veins and as many seeds as you can. Do not remove stems.

2   Stuff about ¾ cup shredded cheese and 3–4 onion strips in each chile. Pin closed with toothpicks if necessary.

3   Separate egg whites and egg yolks. Place yolks in a medium bowl and egg whites in a large mixing bowl. Add salt to egg whites. Beat egg whites with electric mixer on medium speed until stiff peaks form. Beat yolks with a fork and fold into egg whites until well incorporated.

4   Heat oil in a medium frying pan over medium heat.

5   Place flour in a shallow bowl. One at a time, roll each chile in flour, covering all sides. Gently shake off excess flour. Dip chile into egg batter, holding by the stem. Place chile in hot oil and carefully baste with spoonfuls of hot oil until golden brown. Remove from oil and place on paper towel–lined plate to soak up excess oil. Repeat with remaining peppers.

6   To serve, divide tomato sauce between 4 shallow plates. Top with onion slices. Place chiles on tomato sauce and onion slices. Garnish with oregano leaves and a sprinkle of cotija cheese.

Tomato Sauce

PREPARATION TIME: 10 MINUTES
COOKING TIME: 15 MINUTES
MAKES 1 ¾ CUPS

2 tablespoons
canola oil

5 Roma tomatoes,
sliced in half

½ small onion,
sliced in strips

1 large garlic clove,
sliced in half

1 teaspoon salt

½ tablespoon dried
oregano, crushed

1   Heat oil in a large pan over medium heat. Add tomato
    halves, onion strips, and garlic. Cook for 10 minutes,
    turning ingredients frequently with tongs. Do not burn.
    Tomatoes should be soft and skins should begin to peel.

2   Add sautéed tomatoes, onion, and garlic to a blender.
    Add 2 cups water and blend until smooth.

3   Transfer blended mixture back to pan and heat over high
    heat. Season with salt and oregano. Bring to a boil and
    reduce heat to medium. Simmer for 5 minutes. Set aside
    and keep warm.

ENTOMATADAS DE QUESO FRESCO

Queso Fresco Entomatadas

Entomatadas are lightly fried corn tortillas dipped in a savory tomato sauce. Similar to enchiladas, they can be stuffed with shredded cheese, chicken, or ground beef. Although I was a tomato-hater when I was a kid, this meal was and continues to be one of my all-time favorites. Now, entomatadas are part of our weeknight meal rotation. Because they are flavorful but not spicy, they are the perfect kid-friendly "grown-up" meal.

PREPARATION TIME: 20 MINUTES
COOK TIME: 40 MINUTES
MAKES 12

6 large Roma tomatoes, sliced in half lengthwise

¼ cup plus 1 tablespoon olive oil, divided

2 garlic cloves

1 small white onion, chopped and divided

½ teaspoon salt

12 corn tortillas

10 ounces queso fresco, crumbled

¼ cup chopped fresh cilantro

Mexican crema or crème fraîche

1   Heat a large skillet over medium heat. Place tomato halves on hot skillet and roast evenly, turning with tongs, until skins begin to lift and char spots are visible. Remove from heat and let cool. Peel and discard roasted tomato skins.

2   Heat 1 tablespoon oil in a sauté pan over medium heat. Add garlic and ½ chopped onion. Cook, stirring frequently, until onion is translucent, about 3 minutes.

3   Transfer mixture to blender. Add peeled tomatoes. Blend until smooth.

4   Return mixture to sauté pan. Add salt and heat over medium-low heat. Cover. Simmer for 10–12 minutes or until sauce thickens. Remove from heat and let cool.

5   Heat remaining ¼ cup oil over medium heat in a large frying pan. Carefully fry a tortilla for 30 seconds on each side or until tortilla is soft enough to bend. Dip in tomato sauce, evenly covering both sides, and place on a large plate. Fill with 2–3 tablespoons cheese and roll. Arrange on a serving platter with seam side down. Repeat with remaining tortillas, sauce, and cheese. If there is any leftover sauce, drizzle over rolled entomatadas.

6   Serve and top with more cheese, remaining chopped onion, cilantro, and a drizzle of cream.

TAMALITOS LAGUNEROS

Fried Guajillo Masa Cakes

My neighborhood in Torreón was a lively one. During the evening, everyone on our side of the street pulled their chairs outside their front doors. No one had a porch. All the front doors on that street directly led to the sidewalk. My mom, holding my sleeping sister in her arms, chatted with neighbors and enjoyed the cool night breeze. The older kids played soccer on the road, moving aside swiftly as cars drove by; I sat with my friends on the curb to watch. I was about five or six years old.

On the corner of our street lived Lola. She was about fifteen and helped her mom make the most delicious tamalitos lagueros—fried guajillo masa cakes. On Friday evenings, they set up a table right outside their front door covered in large bowls filled with various toppings: shredded cabbage, sliced tomatoes, pickled jalapeños, radish slices, crema, and a very spicy chile de arbol sauce. Lola and her mother fried tamalitos to order in a large disc fryer. The smell was intoxicating and drew a hungry crowd right to their front door.

PREPARATION TIME: 45 MINUTES
COOK TIME: 1 HOUR 15 MINUTES
SERVES 6

5 dried guajillo chiles, rinsed and stems removed

2 dried pasilla chiles, rinsed and stems removed

2 garlic cloves

½ teaspoon whole cumin

3 cups masa harina (corn flour)

2 teaspoons salt

2 teaspoons baking powder

1 cup vegetable oil

TOPPINGS

shredded cabbage

chopped tomato

pickled jalapeños

sliced radishes

Mexican crema or crème fraiche

1   Place dried chiles in a medium saucepan over medium heat with enough water to cover. Simmer for 10 minutes or until chiles soften. Remove from heat and set aside for 5 minutes. Do not throw away water.

2   Place boiled chiles, garlic, cumin, and 2 cups chile water in a blender. Blend until smooth. Set aside and let mixture cool to the touch.

3   Whisk together masa harina, salt, and baking powder in a large bowl. Add guajillo mixture slowly and knead with hands. Add water by the tablespoon if dough is dry. Form a large ball of dough.

4   On a clean, dry surface, divide masa ball into two equal pieces. Form one piece into a cylinder 2 inches in diameter and 4 inches long, like a log. Place it in the center of a 24-inch-long piece of aluminum foil lengthwise. Fold top and bottom pieces of aluminum foil over masa cylinder; pieces must overlap. Fold the four corners inward into triangles, like you would when wrapping a present. Then fold in the two pointy sides to overlap. The idea is to cover the masa completely so minimal water gets in. Repeat with remaining masa.

5   Bring 6 quarts of water to a boil in a large pot over medium heat. Carefully place wrapped masa cylinders in boiling water and cover. Boil for 1 hour or until masa is firm. Remove from heat and let cool. Remove foil and slice masa into 10 discs.

6   Heat oil in a large frying pan over medium heat. Fry 3–4 masa slices at a time, 2 minutes on each side. Transfer to a paper towel–lined plate. Repeat with remaining slices.

7   Immediately serve with cabbage, tomato, pickled jalapeños, radishes, and Mexican crema.

TACOS DE FLOR DE JAMAICA

Hibiscus Tacos

Did you know that hibiscus flowers are edible? Don't throw them out after preparing your agua de Jamaica. Those little blooms can be cooked and added to quesadillas or served on a tostada. I like to wrap them around a warm corn tortilla. The flavor is savory and spicy when topped with pineapple pico de gallo. You can find a refreshing agua de Jamaica recipe in my *Aguas Frescas & Paletas* book.

PREPARATION TIME: 15 MINUTES
COOK TIME 20 MINUTES
SERVES 4

1½ cups dried hibiscus flowers

1 tablespoon olive oil

¼ cup chopped white onion

1 garlic clove, chopped

1 cup chopped Roma tomato

½ teaspoon salt

½ teaspoon black pepper

8 corn tortillas, warmed

pineapple pico de gallo (page 37)

avocado slices for serving

lime slices for serving

1   Bring 3 cups water and hibiscus to a boil in a medium saucepan over medium heat. Boil for 2 minutes. Remove from heat and set aside to seep and cool for 15 minutes. Run mixture through a strainer into a large bowl. Optional: Reserve hibiscus liquid to make agua fresca.

2   Heat olive oil in a large frying pan over medium heat. Add onion and garlic. Sauté for 3–5 minutes or until tender.

3   Add tomato and hibiscus flowers. Cook for 10 minutes, stirring frequently. Season with salt and pepper.

4   Divide mixture on warm corn tortillas. Serve with pineapple pico de gallo and avocado slices. Sprinkle with lime juice, fold, and enjoy.

CALABACITAS RELLENAS DE QUESO PANELA

Panela Cheese-Stuffed Squash

Whenever I prepare a very spicy dish at home, I always find a way to modify that dish and tame down the heat for my son. These panela cheese–stuffed squash came about during a chile relleno prep. The poblanos were very spicy that day, so I decided to create a kid-friendly dish with squash instead. With the addition of the mouthwatering tomato sauce, these little battered squash and panela bites were a big hit.

PREPARATION TIME: 35 MINUTES
COOK TIME: 35 MINUTES
SERVES 4

3 large Mexican squash, sliced in ½-inch rounds

4 eggs

1½ cups plus 1 tablespoon all-purpose flour, divided

5 ounces panela cheese

⅓ cup vegetable oil

tomato sauce for serving (page 143)

1   Place squash slices with enough water to cover in a 4-quart saucepan. Bring to a boil over medium heat. Boil for 5 minutes or until squash slices are tender. Drain and set aside.

2   Separate egg whites from yolks. Place whites in a large mixing bowl. Beat with a hand mixer until soft peaks form. Add yolks. Mix on medium speed for 10 seconds. Add 1 tablespoon flour. Continue mixing until thoroughly combined. Mixture should be thick and creamy.

3   Slice panela cheese in ½-inch-thick slices. Then cut each slice into 1-inch squares. Sandwich each cheese square between two squash slices.

4   Heat oil in a frying pan over medium heat.

5   Place remaining 1½ cups flour in a shallow bowl. One at a time, gently cover each squash sandwich with flour evenly on all sides. Gently shake off excess flour. Dip sandwich into batter, holding squash slices between fingers to keep cheese from falling out. Place sandwich in hot oil and carefully baste with spoonfuls of hot oil until golden brown. Remove from oil and place on paper towel–lined plate to soak up excess oil. Repeat with remaining sandwiches.

6   Serve warm with tomato sauce.

TORTITAS DE PAPA, BRÓCOLI, Y ZANAHORIA CON QUESO COTIJA

Potato, Broccoli, and Carrot Patties with Cotija Cheese

I don't know what it is about these potato, broccoli, and carrot patties, but my son absolutely loves them. They are easy to handle (no silverware!), and the taste of creamy potato mixed in with broccoli and carrot is as kid-friendly as a nugget. Great as appetizers or a box lunch, these veggie-packed treats are fun to prepare as well as devour.

PREPARATION TIME: 20 MINUTES
COOK TIME: 40 MINUTES
MAKES 16

5 small russet potatoes, peeled

1 (12-ounce) package frozen riced broccoli

¼ cup plus 1 tablespoon canola oil, divided

¼ onion, chopped

1 garlic clove, chopped

1½ cups shredded carrot

1½ cups crumbled cotija cheese

1 egg

½ cup panko bread crumbs

⅓ cup all-purpose flour

½ teaspoon salt

½ teaspoon black pepper

1 Roma tomato, chopped

cilantro sprigs for serving

tomato ketchup for dipping

1   Place peeled potatoes in a medium saucepan over medium heat with enough water to cover. Bring to a boil. Boil for 20 minutes or until soft enough to mash. Drain and set aside.

2   Steam broccoli according to package directions. Transfer to a strainer and drain liquid, pressing with a large spoon. Transfer broccoli to a large bowl and set aside to cool.

3   Heat 1 tablespoon oil in a small pan over medium heat. Add onion and garlic. Cook for 3 minutes, until onion is translucent. Set aside.

4   Mash potatoes with potato masher. Add broccoli, sautéed onion and garlic, shredded carrot, cheese, egg, panko bread crumbs, flour, salt, and black pepper. Mix well with hands until a coarse, doughy consistency forms.

5   Heat ¼ cup oil in skillet over medium heat. Scoop ⅓ cup potato mixture into palms of hands and shape into a patty 2 inches in diameter and ½ inch thick. Repeat with the rest of the mixture.

6   Fry patties for 4–6 minutes on each side or until golden brown, adding more oil if necessary. Transfer to a paper towel–lined plate.

7   Serve with chopped tomato, cilantro sprigs, and ketchup.

PASTEL AZTECA DE FLOR DE CALABAZA

Squash Blossom Tortilla Casserole

We have a small garden box in our backyard strictly dedicated for squash and squash blossoms. I get so excited when we get a box full of blooms because I can make this pastel Azteca for my family. Squash and squash blossoms are easy to grow in California weather and are delicious in omelets, as a pizza topping, and especially in this pastel Azteca. Squash blossoms can be found at farmers markets or in the produce section of the Latin supermarket. Grab plenty; they shrink when cooked, just like spinach.

PREPARATION TIME: 20 MINUTES
COOK TIME: 35 MINUTES
SERVES 4–6

½ cup plus 2 tablespoons oil, divided

1 cup chopped white onion

2 large garlic cloves, chopped

1 large Roma tomato, chopped

1 large zucchini, sliced

½ teaspoon salt

¼ teaspoon black pepper

½ teaspoon dried oregano, crushed

3 cups (packed) squash blossom petals, rinsed

6 corn tortillas, cut in half

2 cups grated Oaxaca cheese, divided

1   Heat 2 tablespoons oil in a sauté pan over medium heat. Cook onion and garlic for 2 minutes or until onion begins to soften.

2   Add tomato, zucchini, salt, pepper, and oregano. Stir. Cook for 10 minutes.

3   Add squash blossoms. Cook until blossoms wilt completely, about 2 minutes. Remove from heat and set aside.

4   Preheat oven to 350 degrees.

5   Heat remaining ½ cup oil in a large pan over medium heat. Lightly fry tortilla halves for 30 seconds on each side.

6   Arrange 6 tortilla halves in a 9x6-inch casserole dish. Spoon half the squash blossom mixture evenly over tortillas. Top with 1 cup cheese. Repeat layers: tortillas, squash blossom mixture, cheese. Bake for 15 minutes or until cheese melts completely and begins to bubble.

7   Remove from oven and let cool for 10 minutes. Slice and serve.

TAQUITOS AHOGADOS

Drowned Taquitos

When we visit Mexico City, we make time to visit as many museums as we can. During one of those particular visits in 2017, we ended up in El Parque España famished. We hopped in a taxi and asked the driver to suggest something for us to eat. He said, "*Que no se diga más!*" ("Say no more!") Ten minutes later he dropped us off at the door of a little restaurant called Flautas Ahogadas (Drowned Flutes). They served drowned long crispy tacos resembling a flute in a brothy salsa verde. The tacos were generously topped with a mound of crumbled cotija and ribbons of table cream. Absolute heaven. Here is my version with regular-sized tortillas—drowned potato taquitos.

PREPARATION TIME: 20 MINUTES
COOK TIME: 50 MINUTES
SERVES 4

3 large russet potatoes, peeled

1½ cup shredded asadero or mozzarella cheese

½ teaspoon salt

½ teaspoon pepper

6 tomatillos, husked

1 Roma tomato

¼ cup chopped white onion

1 garlic clove

1½ teaspoons chicken or vegetable bouillon

1 tablespoon olive oil

1 cup vegetable oil

12 corn tortillas, warmed

TOPPINGS

shredded iceberg lettuce

red onion, sliced

Roma tomato, chopped

avocado, sliced

queso fresco

Mexican crema or crème fraîche

lime juice

1   Heat potatoes with enough water to cover in a large saucepan. Boil for 20 minutes or until potatoes are fork-tender. Remove from heat and drain. Mash with a potato masher. Add cheese and season with salt and pepper. Stir to mix well. Set aside.

2   Heat tomatillos and tomato with enough water to cover in a large saucepan over medium heat. Bring to a boil. Decrease heat to low and simmer for 10 minutes.

3   Transfer boiled tomatillos and tomato to a blender. Add onion, garlic, and bouillon. Blend until smooth. Set aside and keep warm.

4   Heat olive oil in a large pan over medium-low heat. Pour in blended sauce and 1 cup water. Simmer for 4 minutes. This is your broth.

5   Heat vegetable oil in a large frying pan over medium-low heat. Spread about 2 tablespoons of potato mixture on tortilla. Roll tightly, secure with a toothpick if needed, and immediately place in hot oil with tongs, seam side down. Fry on all sides until golden brown and crispy. Transfer to a paper towel–lined plate. Repeat with remaining tortillas until all potato mixture has been used.

6   To serve, place 2–3 rolled taquitos in a bowl. Pour in ½ cup broth. Garnish with toppings.

TACOS CRUJIENTES DE FIDEO
Crispy Fideo Tacos

Every time I make crispy fideo tacos, all I hear is *crunch crunch* at the dinner table. Nothing else. These homemade taco shells are filled with guajillo-spiced *fideos secos* (dry noodles) and a thick slice of fresh avocado. Because the fideo seco is made with guajillo chile, its flavor is different from fideo soup (page 87) but still mild enough for kids to enjoy. The fideo seco in this recipe can also be served without the taco shells, casserole style. Your preference. But one thing for sure, make sure you top it with crumbled queso fresco, a drizzle of cream, and a sprinkle of fresh cilantro.

PREPARATION TIME 20 MINUTES
COOK TIME: 35 MINUTES
MAKES 20

3 dried guajillo chiles, stems and seeds removed

4 Roma tomatoes, roughly chopped

2 tablespoons olive oil

200 grams dry fideo pasta

¼ cup chopped white onion

2 garlic cloves, finely chopped

1 teaspoon dried oregano, crushed

1 teaspoon salt

½ teaspoon black pepper

1 cup vegetable or canola oil

20 corn tortillas

TOPPINGS

avocado slices

crumbled queso fresco

Mexican crema or crème fraîche

cilantro

1   Place dried guajillos in a medium saucepan over medium heat with enough water to cover. Simmer for 10 minutes or until chiles soften. Remove from heat and set aside for 5 minutes. Do not throw away water.

2   Add softened chiles, tomatoes, and 1 cup chile water to a blender. Blend until smooth. Set aside.

3   Heat olive oil in a 5-quart saucepan over medium-low heat. Add fideo pasta and stir constantly until pasta is golden brown. Do not burn. Remove from heat and transfer to a separate bowl. Set aside.

4   Return saucepan to medium heat. Sauté onion and garlic until tender, about 1 minute.

5   Add guajillo mixture, oregano, salt, and pepper. Bring to a boil. Add fried fideo. Reduce heat to low. Simmer for 15 minutes or until liquid has been soaked up.

6   While fideo is cooking, prepare taco shells. Heat vegetable oil in large frying pan over medium heat. Test the oil temperature by dipping the edge of a tortilla in the hot oil with a pair of tongs. If the tortilla bubbles rapidly, the oil is ready. Using tongs, carefully fry tortilla in hot oil for 5–7 seconds on each side. Fold tortilla in half using tongs. Fry each side of folded tortilla for 10 seconds or until crispy. Lift taco shell over the oil, letting any excess oil drip off. Place shell on a paper towel–lined plate to absorb any excess oil. Repeat with remaining tortillas.

7   Scoop fideo in taco shells. Add avocado slices, a sprinkle of queso fresco, cream, and cilantro leaves. Serve immediately.

Bebidas
(Drinks)

CAFÉ DE OLLA

Coffee from the Pot

Café de olla literally means "coffee from the pot." Served year-round and best enjoyed with your favorite pan dulce, this sweet and strong drink is said to have originated between 1910 and 1917 during the Mexican Revolution. The *Adelitas*, the women soldiers of the revolution, prepared the beverage with coffee, cinnamon, and piloncillo in a large clay pot. As the drink grew popular through the years, other spices were added. I prefer my cup with a twist of citrus oil from some orange peel for added flavor.

PREPARATION TIME: 5 MINUTES
COOK TIME: 15 MINUTES
REST TIME: 10 MINUTES
SERVES 4

1 orange

6 whole cloves

2 (4-inch) cinnamon sticks, broken up

4 ounces piloncillo

6 tablespoons dark roast ground coffee

4 (1.5-inch-long each) pieces orange peel (optional)

1   Make 6 small punctures in orange with a small paring knife. Insert cloves in each puncture. Set aside.

2   Boil 8½ cups water in a large pot over medium heat. Add orange with cloves, cinnamon sticks, and piloncillo. Simmer for 15 minutes.

3   Stir in coffee and bring to a rapid boil. Turn off heat and let rest for 10 minutes.

4   Run through a strainer and serve.

5   Optional: When serving, twist an orange peel over café de olla to enhance flavor with citrus oil.

AGUA FRESCA DE MELÓN Y ZANAHORIA

Cantaloupe Carrot Agua Fresca

I'm always looking for different and creative for ways to add healthier ingredients into my recipes. This cantaloupe and carrot agua fresca is one of those recipes. *Agua de melón*, cantaloupe cooler (which can be found in my *Aguas Frescas & Paletas* book), is a popular treat, so I enhanced this classic favorite by adding a few carrots to the mix. The carrots not only give this drink a healthy boost but also intensify its color.

◊◊

PREPARATION TIME: 15 MINUTES
SERVES 8–10

8 cups water, divided

½ cup sugar

½ cantaloupe, seeds removed and pulp chopped

3 medium carrots, peeled and roughly chopped

2 key limes, juiced

1   Combine 6 cups water and sugar in a large pitcher. Stir until sugar dissolves. Set aside.

2   Combine cantaloupe, carrots, and remaining 2 cups water in a blender. Blend until smooth. Run mixture through a strainer into pitcher, pressing pulp with a spoon to release as much liquid as possible.

3   Stir in lime juice. Serve over ice.

CHILATE
Cacao, Rice, and Cinnamon Chilate

Preparing chilate is an experience for the senses all on its own, from toasting the cacao beans to peeling them to taking in the aroma of pulverized cinnamon sticks with soaked rice. It's almost romantic when you see the paste you just created become a delicious drink. Cacao beans can be found in specialty stores or online.

PREPARATION TIME: 1 HOUR 50 MINUTES
COOK TIME: 7 MINUTES
SERVES 6

1⅓ cups dry white rice, rinsed

2 (4-inch) cinnamon sticks, broken up in pieces

2 cups unpeeled cacao beans

6 ounces piloncillo, grated

1   Combine rice, cinnamon, and 3 cups water in a large bowl. Soak for 1 hour.

2   While rice and cinnamon soak, heat a large skillet or comal over medium heat. Add cacao beans and slowly stir with a wooden spoon. Toast for 5–7 minutes or until beans pop and dark brown spots appear. Remove from heat and transfer to a large plate to cool completely. Peel beans.

3   Add peeled cacao beans to container with rice and cinnamon. Soak for an additional 10 minutes.

4   Strain mixture and transfer to blender or food processor. Blend until a paste forms. Add ½ cup water if needed to help paste consistency form.

5   Transfer paste to a large bowl. Add 6 cups water and stir until paste breaks up and thins out. Strain mixture 3 times into a large pitcher.

6   Add piloncillo and stir to dissolve. Serve over ice. To obtain the foamy consistency when serving, raise the pitcher approximately 20 inches above the serving glass when pouring.

CHOCOLATE DE AGUA

Water-Based Mexican Hot Chocolate

Enjoy your churros (page 186) or pan de rancho (page 201) with a cup of frothy chocolate de agua. Different from the milk-based Mexican hot chocolate, chocolate de agua is water-based, therefore thinner but with a richer, bittersweet flavor of chocolate. This is a great drink to dunk your favorite pan dulce in.

PREPARATION TIME: 5 MINUTES
COOK TIME: 10 MINUTES
SERVES 4

4 cups water
1 (4-inch) cinnamon stick

1 (90-gram) tablet Mexican chocolate

1   Combine water, cinnamon stick, and chocolate tablet in a medium saucepan over medium heat. Stir until chocolate dissolves, about 10 minutes.

2   Use a *molinillo* (see page 7) or frother to make froth by holding handle between palms and rotating by rubbing palms together. Serve immediately.

CHILEATOLE VERDE
Green Chileatole

Chileatole is a thick but smooth drink that has indigenous roots. Its name in Nahuatl, *chilli* and *atolli*, mean "chile" and "atole." (Atole is a traditional hot corn and masa–based drink). Therefore, it is considered a beverage. But seeing how this "drink" is prepared, with many people adding chicken or pork and vegetables, it is also recognized as a stew.

There are many variations of this cozy treat across Mexican kitchens. This one is mine.

PREPARATION TIME: 15 MINUTES
COOK TIME: 1 HOUR 10 MINUTES
SERVES 12

6 cups white corn, rinsed

6 fresh epazote sprigs, divided

2 teaspoons salt

1 cup corn flour

1 small poblano chile, seeds removed, chopped

1 jalapeño, seeds removed, chopped

1 cup fresh spinach

1 cup fresh radish leaves

TOPPINGS

crumbled queso fresco

sliced serrano chiles

lime juice

1   Combine 10 cups water, corn, 2 epazote sprigs, and salt in a large pot over medium heat. Bring to a boil. Cook about 10 minutes.

2   Whisk together 1 cup water and corn flour. Mixture should be thick and smooth. Add to boiling pot and stir.

3   Combine 1 cup water, remaining 4 epazote sprigs, poblano chile, jalapeño, spinach, and radish leaves in a blender. Blend until smooth. Add to boiling pot and stir.

4   Decrease heat to medium-low. Cover and cook for 1 hour, stirring frequently to avoid clumping.

5   Serve. Top with cheese or serrano chiles (optional) and a sprinkle of lime juice.

TÉ DE FLOR DE JAMAICA CON JENGIBRE

Hibiscus Flower Tea with Ginger

I love hibiscus tea over ice, but on a cold day, a hot cup of this tea is comforting. The antioxidants from the blooms and the digestive benefits of ginger make for a delicious and soothing elixir.

PREPARATION TIME: 10 MINUTES
COOK TIME: 5 MINUTES
SERVES 2

2 cups water

½ cup dried hibiscus blooms

1 tablespoon chopped fresh ginger

1   Combine ingredients in a small saucepan over medium heat. Boil for 5 minutes. Remove from heat and let steep for 7–10 minutes.

2   Pour tea through a strainer into two teacups. Sweeten with your favorite sweetener. Serve hot or over ice.

AGUA FRESCA DE MANGO

Mango Agua Fresca

There is a gentleman fruit vendor I always look for when I exit the freeway near my home. He walks up and down the median with sacks of oranges and crates of seasonal fruit. On special days, and if I'm lucky to drive by early enough, he will have boxes of Ataulfo mangos for sale. They are perfectly arranged, like fragile golden eggs, and I'm ecstatic to take a box home.

I could easily say the Ataulfo mango is the most delicious fruit in the entire world. It's like custard; its buttery honey flavor is near perfection. It's the ideal fruit to easily peel and eat right out of your hand. Because it's not as fibrous as other mango varieties, it is used in many Mexican dishes and aguas frescas. Here's one of my favorite ways to use those beautiful mangos. If you don't have a favorite street fruit vendor, get them at your nearest grocery stores February to early August.

PREPARATION TIME: 10 MINUTES
SERVES 6

4 cups water

2 cups mango pulp (about 4 Ataulfo mangos)

⅓ cup lime juice

½ cup sugar

lime wedges for garnish

chile lime powder for garnish

mint sprigs for garnish

1   Combine 4 cups water, mango pulp, lime juice, and sugar in a blender. Blend until smooth. Transfer mixture to a pitcher.

2   Run a lime wedge along rim of the glasses or cups you'll be using. Dip glass rim in chile lime powder. Add ice and serve. Garnish with lime wedges and mint sprigs.

AGUA DE HORCHATA CON PALETAS DE TUNA ROJA

Horchata with Red Prickly Pear Pops

Traditional horchata is served topped with red prickly pear syrup. Some include chunks of cantaloupe, roasted pepitas, and chopped pecans. I gave my traditional horchata recipe a modern twist by freezing sweet prickly pear syrup into a vibrant *paleta* (popsicle). The paleta slowly melts while keeping your horchata cool with hot pink syrup swirls. To give it a little bit of a crunch, I added chopped pecans and pomegranate arils.

PREPARATION TIME: 20 MINUTES
CHILL TIME: 4 HOURS TO OVERNIGHT
SOAK TIME: 4 HOURS TO OVERNIGHT
SERVES 6

Red Prickly Pear Pops

5 red prickly pears, peeled

2 tablespoons granulated sugar

1 tablespoon lime juice

1   Place prickly pears in a blender. Blend until smooth. Run through a mesh strainer into a container with a spout. Add sugar and lime juice and stir until sugar dissolves. Divide mixture into 6 popsicle molds, insert sticks, and chill for at least 4 hours.

Horchata

1 cup dry white rice

1 (4-inch) cinnamon stick

6 cups water, divided

⅔ cup sugar

pomegranate arils for topping

chopped pecans for topping

2   Combine rice, cinnamon stick, and 2 cups water in a large bowl. Cover with plastic wrap and let soak overnight.

3   Place rice and water mixture with cinnamon stick in a blender. Blend until smooth. Run through a mesh strainer into a large pitcher. Add remaining 4 cups water and sugar and stir.

4   To serve, place a few ice cubes in a serving glass. Add horchata, filling halfway. Then carefully add popsicle. Garnish with pomegranate arils and chopped pecans.

Postres
(Desserts)

ALEGRÍAS
Amaranth Candy

Alegrías, meaning "joys," are a popular Mexican candy made of puffed amaranth bound together with a sweetener such as honey, sugar, or piloncillo. Alegrías are just what they say they are—a joy to have, as they are light, crispy, and perfectly sweet. You will find these delicate treats wrapped in clear cellophane sheets all over Mexico. They're sold by street vendors and in candy stores in busy areas of downtown or popular touristy spots. Some alegrías are plain, and others are decorated with various seeds, nuts, and dried fruit. Puffed amaranth can be found online or in specialty stores.

PREPARATION TIME: 10 MINUTES
COOK TIME: 20 MINUTES
SET TIME: AT LEAST 2 HOURS
SERVES 8

2 tablespoons roasted pepitas

¼ cup pecan halves, roasted

¼ cup almonds, roasted

½ tablespoon sesame seeds, roasted

¼ cup raisins

3 cups puffed amaranth

1 (6-ounce) piloncillo cone, roughly chopped

1 tablespoon lime juice

⅓ cup raw honey

1   Line an 8-inch square baking pan with wax paper. Arrange pepitas, pecans, almonds, sesame seeds, and raisins on prepared pan. Set aside.

2   Place amaranth in a large saucepan over medium heat. Toast for 4–5 minutes, stirring frequently. The amaranth will darken slightly in color. Do not burn. Immediately transfer to a large bowl.

3   Combine piloncillo, lime juice, honey, and 1 cup water in a large saucepan over medium heat. Cook for 13–15 minutes or until mixture is thick.

4   Turn heat off and immediately add amaranth to piloncillo syrup. Fold mixture quickly and thoroughly with a silicone spatula, making sure syrup is evenly distributed.

5   Transfer to lined baking dish over nuts and seeds. Press with spatula, then press with dampened hands. Mixture must be compact and even. At this point, with mixture still warm and soft, slice amaranth into 8 pieces with a wet knife. This will make the pieces break apart with ease once mixture has hardened.

6   Let mixture cool and harden completely for at least 2 hours. Break pieces apart or use a wet knife to detach completely.

ARROZ CON LECHE CON CAJETA Y COCO

Rice Pudding with Cajeta and Coconut

My mom's arroz con leche is a special treat. The aroma of simmering cinnamon and whole cloves permeates the kitchen and envelops me, no matter how old I am, like a warm hug. I like to enjoy it as soon as it's ready, steaming hot with plump, tender raisins, a drizzle of cajeta (or dulce de leche), and a sprinkle of toasted coconut.

◇◇

PREPARATION TIME: 20 MINUTES
COOK TIME: 30 MINUTES
SERVES 4–6

I cup long-grain rice

I (4-inch) cinnamon stick

3 whole cloves

2 cups milk

I cup evaporated milk

½ cup sugar

½ cup raisins

cajeta for drizzling

toasted coconut for topping

1   Soak rice in 2 cups water for 20 minutes. Drain.

2   Combine 3 cups water, cinnamon stick, and cloves in a large saucepan over medium heat. Bring to a boil. Add rice. Reduce heat to medium-low. Simmer until water has been mostly absorbed and rice is tender but not dry, about 15–20 minutes.

3   Stir in milks, sugar, and raisins. Simmer for 5 minutes. Remove from heat and let cool and thicken.

4   Scoop rice pudding in serving dishes. Drizzle with cajeta and top with toasted coconut.

BESITOS DE NUEZ
Pecan Kisses

On my wedding day, all the guests were admiring not the bride (me), not the dress, not the flowers, but the cookies. Those cookies—also known as *besitos de nuez*, *bizcochitos*, or Mexican wedding cookies—have been one of the most cherished wedding gifts I received that day. They were made by my aunt Petty, who's known for making the most delicate melt-in-your-mouth besitos de nuez. Some of the cookies were rolled into cherry-sized balls, others were cut into diamond shapes, all were topped with a pecan half, and last but certainly not least, each cookie was dusted with either confectioners' sugar or cinnamon sugar. People still talk about those cookies to this day.

PREPARATION TIME: 40 MINUTES
COOK TIME: 20 MINUTES
MAKES 45–48

1 cup butter, room temperature	**CINNAMON SUGAR TOPPING**	**POWDERED SUGAR TOPPING**
2 teaspoons vanilla extract		
¼ cup granulated sugar	½ cup granulated sugar	½ cup powdered sugar
1 cup finely chopped pecans	1 teaspoon ground cinnamon	
2 cups all-purpose flour		

1   Preheat oven to 350 degrees. Line two baking trays with parchment paper. Set aside.

2   Place butter in the bowl of a stand mixer. Mix at medium speed. When butter is creamy, gradually add vanilla and sugar. Decrease speed and add pecans and flour. Continue mixing until dough is formed.

3   Scoop out 1 tablespoon of dough. Roll dough into a ball. Place on prepared baking sheet. Repeat with remaining dough, placing balls about 2 inches apart.

4   Bake for 20 minutes or until bottoms of cookies are golden brown. Remove from oven and allow to cool slightly.

5   Mix granulated sugar and cinnamon in a shallow bowl. Place powdered sugar in a separate shallow bowl.

6   While cookies are still warm (not hot), roll half the cookies in cinnamon sugar and the other half in powdered sugar. Coat evenly.

7   Transfer to wire rack and cool completely. Store in a tightly sealed container.

CHURROS CON CREMA DE ROMPOPE

Churros with Rompope Cream Sauce

The first time I made homemade churros, I felt like I had revealed a long-kept Mexican pastry-making secret. The process is simple, and just like everything else, the more you practice making them, the better the result. I recommend using a pastry piping bag with a star tip, but you can also use a large, thick plastic bag with the tip cut out. Be careful when piping as the dough tends to be dense and takes a bit of strength to squeeze.

    Enjoy these homemade churros with a boozy rompope cream sauce. Rompope can be found at your local liquor store or your Latin grocery in the liquor section. It is an egg-based vanilla drink that contains rum. For a kid-friendly version, omit rompope cream sauce; you could also serve the churros with melted chocolate.

PREPARATION TIME: 20 MINUTES
COOK TIME: 30 MINUTES
SET TIME: 1 HOUR
MAKES 22–24 (4-INCH) CHURROS

1 (4-inch) cinnamon stick

¾ cup plus 2 tablespoons granulated sugar, divided

1 teaspoon salt

1 teaspoon vanilla extract

½ cup butter

2 cups all-purpose flour, sifted

2 eggs, beaten

vegetable or canola oil for frying

1   Combine 2 cups plus 2 tablespoons water and cinnamon stick in a large saucepan over medium heat. Boil for 10 minutes. Remove and discard cinnamon stick.

2   Add 2 tablespoons sugar, salt, and vanilla to boiling water. Stir. When sugar has dissolved, add butter and stir to melt.

3   Remove saucepan from heat. Add flour. Stir with a wooden spoon until a smooth dough forms and does not stick to saucepan. Add eggs and continue stirring with wooden spoon until ingredients have mixed thoroughly to create a thick, smooth dough.

4   Transfer dough to a pastry piping bag fitted with a 1M star tip. Place remaining ¾ cup sugar on a shallow plate.

5   Add oil ½ inch deep to a large frying pan. Heat over medium heat. Carefully pipe a 4-inch churro in hot oil. Working in batches of 2 or 3 churros, fry on both sides until golden brown, about 2 minutes on each side. Using a spatula, transfer to a paper towel–lined plate to drain for 1 minute. Coat churros with sugar evenly on all sides while still warm.

Rompope Cream Sauce

MAKES ¾ CUP

½ tablespoon
  unflavored gelatin

⅔ cup heavy
  whipping cream

⅔ cup sweetened
  condensed milk

⅔ cup rompope

1   Whisk together 2 tablespoons warm water and gelatin
    until gelatin dissolves.

2   In a separate small bowl, combine cream, sweetened
    condensed milk, and rompope.

3   Add gelatin mixture and whisk to mix well. Refrigerate
    for 1 hour or until sauce thickens.

BARRA DE CONCHA

Concha Loaf

I first experienced a barra de concha at El Cardenal Restaurant in Mexico City. The presentation was impressive. After oohing and aahing, everyone took a turn, sliced their own piece like a cake, and enjoyed it with their very own cup of *chocolate de agua*, a water-based Mexican hot chocolate (page 168).

Inspired by that wonderful experience, I created my own barra de concha at home and prepared a loaf as an ending to a special occasion. It's festive, fun to serve, and, best of all, big enough to enjoy the next day with a *cafecito*.

PREPARATION TIME: 30 MINUTES
REST TIME: 3 HOURS 10 MINUTES
COOK TIME: 27 MINUTES
SERVES 12

2 cups all-purpose flour plus more for kneading

½ cup plus ½ teaspoon granulated sugar, divided

¼ cup butter, softened

2 eggs, divided

⅛ teaspoon salt

2 tablespoons vanilla extract

⅓ cup plus ¼ cup milk, divided

1 (7-gram) packet active dry yeast

1 teaspoon vegetable oil

TOPPING

½ cup butter

½ cup flour

½ cup confectioners' sugar

2 tablespoons cacao powder

1. Place 2 cups flour on a working surface. Make a well in the middle and add ¼ cup sugar, butter, 1 egg, and salt. Mix by hand.

2. Add second egg and vanilla. Dough will be sticky. Knead by hand until dough begins to dry. Slowly add ⅓ cup milk and continue kneading by hand until dough is smooth.

3. Warm ¼ cup milk to about 100 degrees. Combine yeast, warm milk, and ½ teaspoon sugar in a small bowl. Gently stir with a spoon. Transfer to a warm place. Let stand until yeast turns foamy, about 10 minutes.

4. Stretch out dough on working surface. Add remaining ¼ cup sugar and knead until the sugar is completely distributed.

5. Make an indentation in the middle of the dough with your fist. Add yeast mixture. Knead. Dough will become sticky. Continue kneading until dough is smooth and elastic. If needed, sprinkle 1–2 teaspoons of flour on dough. Roll into a large ball.

6. Oil a large bowl with vegetable oil. Transfer dough to bowl, cover with plastic wrap, and place in a warm area for 2½ hours or until dough doubles in size. Deflate dough with fingers, cover, and let stand for another 10 minutes.

7. While dough rises, prepare topping. Place butter in a large bowl. Mix with hand mixer until creamy. Add flour and sugar. Continue mixing. Remove half the mixture and place in a separate bowl. Add cacao powder to the first mixing bowl and continue mixing until chocolate paste forms. Divide each paste into 3 balls (6 balls total). Press each ball into ¼-inch-thick discs.

8. Transfer bread dough to working surface. Roll into a 20-inch loaf. Transfer to a large parchment paper–lined baking sheet. Lightly press each disc paste on loaf, alternating colors and making sure entire top and sides of loaf are covered. Dust a small knife with flour and cut a crosshatch pattern on topping. Cover with plastic wrap, place in a warm place, and let loaf rise for 30 minutes or until it doubles in size.

9. Preheat oven to 400 degrees. Place loaf in oven and reduce heat to 350 degrees. Bake for 25–27 minutes or until bread is golden brown. Cool on a wire rack. Slice and serve.

HELADO DE PAPAYA CON TOTOPOS DE CHURRO

Creamy Papaya Ice Cream with Churro Crisps

When papayas are in season, they sit in the produce section and call my name all summer long. They're huge and enticing. I enjoy them drenched in honey with my yogurt, in a green salad with a vinaigrette dressing, and in an agua fresca loaded with ice and a twist of lime juice. A papaya goes a long way, and I've found many ways to use up every last piece. This creamy papaya ice cream is my favorite way.

I like to think that I survive summers thanks to this ice cream. It's such a decadence to me because it's so rich and refreshing. I like to serve it with churro crisps for an added cinnamon-sugar crunch.

SERVES 8–10

Creamy Papaya Ice Cream

PREPARATION TIME: 10 MINUTES • CHILL TIME: 4 HOURS

4 cups chopped papaya	2 cups heavy whipping cream
1 (14-ounce) can sweetened condensed milk	2 teaspoons vanilla extract

1   Combine all ingredients in a blender. Blend on high for 1 minute or until mixture thickens. Pour mixture into an 8-inch square container and cover with plastic wrap. Chill in freezer for at least 4 hours or until set.

2   To serve, remove ice cream from freezer and let thaw for 5–10 minutes. Scoop into serving dishes and garnish with churro crisps.

Churro Crisps

PREPARATION TIME: 10 MINUTES • COOK TIME: 15 MINUTES

½ cup vegetable oil	2 tablespoons granulated sugar
2 large flour tortillas, sliced in triangles	½ tablespoon ground cinnamon

1   Heat oil in a large frying pan over medium heat. Fry tortilla triangles a few at a time, turning carefully with tongs, until golden.

2   Stir together sugar and cinnamon in a shallow dish. Coat fried tortillas with cinnamon sugar evenly on both sides. Transfer to a paper towel–lined plate to cool for serving.

FRESAS CON CREMA

Strawberries and Cream

Go to any ice cream or *raspa* (shaved ice) shops in Mexico and you will find fresas con crema on the menu. This popular dessert has also been transformed into *paletas* (popsicles) and agua fresca drinks. The sweet cream is the perfect milky combination to complement fresh strawberries. It's best served cold on a hot summer day.

PREPARATION TIME: 15 MINUTES
CHILL TIME: 1 HOUR
SERVES 10

5 cups strawberries

1 cup heavy whipping cream

½ cup Mexican cream or crème fraîche

½ cup sweetened condensed milk

1 teaspoon vanilla

¼ teaspoon cinnamon powder

1   Rinse, hull, and slice strawberries into fourths.

2   Place heavy whipping cream in a large mixing bowl. Whip with electric mixer or with a fork until soft peaks form.

3   Fold in remaining ingredients and strawberries. Refrigerate for 1 hour before serving.

MANTECADAS

Mexican Muffins

My grandmother lived directly behind her *miscelánea* shop, and mornings at dawn meant a daily bread delivery. The most popular pan dulce—*conchas*, *campechanas*, pineapple empanadas, and *mantecadas*—were always part of that delivery. With sleepy eyes and bed head, I was always ready to open the door for the whistle-happy *panadero*. As I held the door open, he always handed me a warm, vanilla-scented mantecada for me to enjoy while he proudly arranged the day's bread in the glass display case.

Mantecadas are a classic spongy muffin-like pan dulce, customarily baked in their characteristic red liner. There are many versions of this pastry. *Manteca* (lard or shortening), where their name derives from, can be substituted with butter or oil. My personal preference is vegetable oil.

PREPARATION TIME: 15 MINUTES
COOK TIME: 20 MINUTES
MAKES 24

2 cups all-purpose flour	1 cup plus 2 tablespoons granulated sugar
¼ teaspoon salt	⅔ cup whole milk, room temperature
1 tablespoon baking powder	1 teaspoon vanilla extract
5 eggs	¼ cup vegetable oil

1   Preheat oven to 390 degrees. Line 2 standard muffin tins with cupcake liners.

2   Sift flour, salt, and baking powder into a large bowl. Whisk together and set aside.

3   Combine eggs and sugar in a bowl of a stand mixer. Mix at medium speed with whisk attachment until thick and creamy, about 5 minutes. Increase speed to high and mix 5 minutes more. Mixture will be fluffy.

4   Continue mixing at high speed. Slowly add milk and vanilla. Decrease speed to medium. Add dry ingredients in ½ cup increments, letting them mix completely between increments. Add oil in a slow stream. Increase mixing speed to high and mix for 1 minute.

5   Divide batter evenly in prepared muffin tins. Bake for 10 minutes. Decrease oven temperature to 350 degrees and bake for 10 minutes more or until golden brown; when tested with a toothpick, the toothpick should come out clean. Remove from oven and let cool in muffin tin.

PEPITORIA
Pumpkin Seed Candy

Go to any *mercado* in Mexico and you'll be sure to find a candy stand filled to the brim with baskets of colorful candy of all kinds. *Pepitoria*—a *pepita* (pumpkin seed) candy molded into slabs with melted sugar or piloncillo—is one of the most popular. Also known as *palanquetas*, these beautiful textured candies are wrapped in clear cellophane ready to be gifted to a loved one. Similar to peanut brittle, pepitoria is thin and crispy, easy to snap and share—but only if you really want to.

PREPARATION TIME: 5 MINUTES
COOK TIME: 10 MINUTES
REST TIME: 2 HOURS
SERVES 4–6

I cup granulated sugar

I ½ cups roasted unsalted pepitas

I teaspoon vanilla extract

1   Line a 9x13-inch baking sheet or dish with parchment paper. Spray (or butter) parchment paper with nonstick cooking spray.

2   Place sugar in a medium nonstick saucepan over medium heat. Stir slowly with a large wooden spoon until sugar melts and color changes to a dark amber, about 5 minutes.

3   Decrease heat to low. Fold in pepitas and vanilla extract.

4   Carefully transfer mixture to lined baking tray. Spray (or butter) the back of a metal spoon. Using the back of the spoon, spread seed mixture into an even ½-inch-thick layer. Set aside to cool and set, about 2 hours.

5   Spray (or butter) the blade of a large knife. Chop pepita candy into serving or bite-size portions.

CAPIROTADA DE COCO Y PLÁTANO

Coconut Banana Capirotada

Some say *capirotada* (Mexican bread pudding) was invented as a way to use up leftovers before beginning the Lenten fast. For many, it is also a way to include protein in meals in the form of cheese, since meat is forbidden during Holy Week and Fridays leading up to Easter.

There really is no proclaimed authentic capirotada that I know of. Every Mexican family has its own version, but there are a few key ingredients that must be included. Without stale bread, piloncillo syrup, and cheese, it just isn't Mexican capirotada. Many include tomatoes, onions, and even tortillas, adding to its rich and delicious complexity.

Making this version of capirotada with coconut and banana is my new twist to this classic dish. The combination makes it into something decadent but not overly sweet. Just perfect.

PREPARATION TIME: 15 MINUTES
COOK TIME: 35 MINUTES
SERVES 12

6 bolillos or large French rolls, sliced

2 tablespoons butter

2 (13.5-ounce) cans coconut milk

1 (8-ounce) cone piloncillo

1 (4-inch) cinnamon stick

¼ cup cream of coconut

½ cup sweetened coconut shreds, divided

½ cup sliced almonds, divided

½ cup raisins, divided

1 cup cubed Oaxaca cheese, divided

2 bananas, sliced, divided

2 tablespoons nonpareils or sprinkles

1   Preheat oven to 350 degrees. Spray a 10x10-inch baking dish with nonstick cooking spray. Set aside.

2   Arrange bread slices on a baking sheet. Brush with butter on both sides. Bake for 12 minutes or until golden brown, flipping halfway through. Remove from oven and set aside.

3   Combine coconut milk, piloncillo, and cinnamon stick in a medium saucepan over medium-low heat. Bring to a simmer and stir until piloncillo dissolves. Remove from heat and stir in cream of coconut until it dissolves.

4   Spoon about ¼ cup coconut milk mixture in prepared baking dish, covering the bottom. Using tongs, dip half the toasted bread in saucepan with coconut milk mixture. Cover bread completely and let each slice soak up liquid for about 5 seconds. Arrange on baking dish as a single layer.

5   Top with ¼ cup shredded coconut, ¼ cup sliced almonds, ¼ cup raisins, ½ cup Oaxaca cheese, and 1 sliced banana.

6   Repeat with a second bread layer and remaining toppings except banana. Cover with aluminum foil. Bake for 10 minutes.

7   Top with any leftover coconut milk and remaining banana slices. Cover and bake for another 5 minutes.

8   Sprinkle with nonpareils. Let cool for 10 minutes. Serve.

PAN DE RANCHO
Ranch Bread

"Para chopear!" ("To dunk!") is what my grandmother used to say when she planned on baking this pan de rancho. We didn't consider it a pan dulce. It is more of a dinner roll to enjoy as an accompaniment to your meal. With just a "brush" of piloncillo syrup on top, this soft and spongy bread becomes the perfect dunking partner (*para chopear*) to your chocolate de agua (page 168).

PREPARATION TIME: 35 MINUTES
REST TIME: I HOUR 25 MINUTES
BAKE TIME: 25 MINUTES
MAKES 27–32

- 2 cups warm water (110 degrees), divided
- I cup plus 2 tablespoons granulated sugar, divided
- 3 (7-ounce) packets active dry yeast

- 8 cups all-purpose flour plus more for kneading
- I teaspoon salt
- 1½ cups vegetable shortening, room temperature
- I teaspoon vegetable oil, divided

PILONCILLO SYRUP

- ½ cup water
- I large cinnamon stick
- 3 ounces piloncillo

I   Place I cup warm water in a medium bowl. Add 2 tablespoons sugar. Stir to dissolve. Gently stir in yeast with a spoon. Transfer to a warm place. Let stand until yeast turns foamy, about 10–15 minutes.

2   Sift flour and salt onto a working surface. Add remaining I cup sugar and shortening. Mix with hands to resemble coarse sand. Add yeast mix and remaining cup warm water. Mix with hands until ingredients are completely incorporated and texture is sticky.

3   Rub ½ teaspoon oil on the surface of a large bowl. Transfer dough to the oiled bowl. Cover with plastic wrap and set aside in warm area for 45 minutes or until dough doubles in size. Deflate dough with fingers. Cover and let stand for 10 minutes.

4   Line two large baking sheets with parchment paper.

5   Divide dough in half. Sprinkle some flour on working surface and transfer half of dough to working surface. Oil hands with remaining ½ teaspoon oil. Roll dough on working surface until you have a 12-inch-long loaf. Repeat with remaining half of dough.

6   Slice each loaf into 14–16 pieces. Shape each piece into a 2½-inch ball. Place on prepared baking sheet and press down with palm of hand to slightly flatten into discs. You will have approximately 27–32 dough discs in total. Cover with plastic wrap and set aside in a warm area for 30 minutes.

7   While dough discs rise, preheat oven to 350 degrees. Once dough has risen, bake for 25 minutes or until golden brown.

8   While bread bakes, prepare piloncillo syrup. Combine water, cinnamon stick, and piloncillo in a medium saucepan. Dissolve piloncillo and bring to a boil. Boil for 5 minutes. Remove from heat and let cool. Mixture will thicken slightly.

9   Once bread is done, immediately brush tops with piloncillo syrup. Set aside to cool. Serve with chocolate de agua.

PASTEL DE TRES LECHES
Tres Leches Cake

This is my favorite cake. It's the first cake my mom taught me to bake and the cake I choose every year to celebrate my birthday with. A tres leches cake is a vanilla sponge-like cake soaked with a mixture of three different types of milk: evaporated milk, sweetened condensed milk, and table (or heavy) cream. The cake is light and airy and keeps its shape despite soaking up all that milk. Many bakers add rum or brandy to the mix, but that is completely up to you.

PREPARATION TIME: 40 MINUTES • SERVES 12
BAKE TIME: 35 MINUTES • CHILL TIME: OVERNIGHT

1¼ cups all-purpose flour

1½ teaspoons baking powder

6 large eggs, room temperature

¾ cup granulated sugar

2 teaspoons vanilla extract

3 tablespoons vegetable oil

2 cups strawberries for topping

MILK MIXTURE

1 (12-ounce) can evaporated milk

1 (14-ounce) can sweetened condensed milk

1 (7.6-ounce) can table cream or 1 cup heavy cream

1 teaspoon vanilla extract

¼ cup dark rum or brandy (optional)

FROSTING

1⅓ cups heavy whipping cream

3 tablespoons confectioners' sugar

1 teaspoon vanilla extract

1   Preheat oven to 340 degrees. Line the bottom of a 9-inch springform pan with parchment paper and spray with nonstick cooking spray. Set aside.

2   Sift flour and baking powder into a medium bowl. Set aside.

3   Combine eggs and sugar in the bowl of stand mixer. Mix with whisk attachment at medium speed for 30 seconds. Then increase speed to high. When mixture begins to fluff, add vanilla extract. Continue mixing at high speed for 10–12 minutes or until mixture has tripled in size.

4   Sift flour and baking powder again, ½ cup at a time, into wet mixture, gently folding in with a spatula between each addition. Then gently fold in oil in a slow stream. Continue folding until all ingredients have mixed well.

5   Pour mixture into prepared pan. Bake for 30–35 minutes until a wooden skewer or small knife used to test comes out clean. Let cool in pan for 10 minutes on a cooling rack.

6   Run a small knife around the edges of pan. Release the side of the springform pan and remove the base. Do not remove parchment paper. Let the cake cool completely on the cooling rack.

7   While cake cools, make the milk mixture. Whisk together milks and cream, vanilla extract, and rum or brandy (optional) in a large bowl. Set aside.

8   Line the same springform pan, with parchment paper still on, with two (24-inch-long) sheets of plastic wrap, letting edges of sheets hang off the sides. Transfer cake to lined pan. Poke holes in the top of the cake with a wooden skewer or fork.

9   Ladle milk mixture on cake, letting it absorb between scoops. Cover with the edges of plastic wrap and refrigerate overnight.

10   Unmold cake on a serving platter. Remove parchment paper and plastic wrap. Set aside.

11   To make frosting, place heavy whipping cream in the bowl of a stand mixer. Mix with whisk attachment on medium-high for 1 minute or until cream begins to fluff. Add sugar and vanilla. Increase speed to high until stiff peaks form.

12   Frost cake with a thin spatula. Decorate with strawberries. Slice and serve.

RASPADO DE SANDÍA

Watermelon Shaved Ice

A *raspado* or *raspa* literally means "scrape" or "scraped." Not to be confused with a snow cone, raspados are made with fresh fruit juice, nothing artificial. Raspa stands are popular in the streets of Mexico in the summertime. Many are set up in residential areas right outside front doors. A large block of ice and bottles of fruit juice or syrup are set up on an oilcloth-protected makeshift table. The more elaborate desserts are topped with fresh fruit, condensed milk, tamarind candy, or chile powder.

PREPARATION TIME: 15 MINUTES
CHILL TIME: 4 HOURS TO OVERNIGHT
SERVES 4–6

8 cups chopped watermelon

4 key limes, juiced

½ cup granulated sugar

chile lime powder or chile powder for serving

mint sprigs for garnish

1   Combine watermelon, lime juice, and sugar in a blender. Blend until smooth.

2   Pour mixture into a plastic or metal container with lid or cover with plastic wrap. Chill in freezer for 2 hours.

3   Remove container from freezer. Scrape mixture with fork thoroughly. Cover and return to freezer for 1 hour.

4   Remove container from freezer. Scrape mixture with fork again. Cover and return to freezer for 1 hour or until mixture has frozen completely.

5   Scoop into serving cups. Garnish with chile lime salt or chile powder and a mint sprig.

GELATINA DE NARANJA Y DURAZNO

Orange and Peach Gelatin

Seeing a decorative gelatina at a party or Easter celebration always brings a smile to my face. I love making layered gelatins with at least one creamy and sweet layer. This orange and peach gelatin is my favorite flavor combination and one of the easiest to make. If canned peaches are not available, try it with canned mandarin wedges and maraschino cherries. It's festive, it serves as a table centerpiece, and it's delicious.

PREPARATION TIME: 15 MINUTES
CHILL TIME: 4 HOURS 40 MIN TO OVERNIGHT
SERVES 12

1 (3-ounce) package orange gelatin

3 cups boiling water, divided

1½ cups cold water, divided

1 (6-ounce) package orange or peach flavor gelatin

2 (0.25-ounce each) gelatin packets

1 (7.9-ounce) can table cream

¾ cup sweetened condensed milk

1 (15-ounce) can peaches in fruit juice, drained

1 Place 3 ounces flavored gelatin in a heatproof container. Add 1 cup boiling water and stir until gelatin dissolves. Add ½ cup cold water and stir to mix. Set aside. This is the plain gelatin.

2 In a separate heatproof container, place 6 ounces flavored gelatin and 2 packets unflavored gelatin. Add remaining 2 cups boiling water and stir until gelatins completely dissolve. Stir in table cream and condensed milk. Add remaining 1 cup cold water and stir until all ingredients are combined and no gelatin lumps are visible. This is the creamy gelatin.

3 Spray mold with nonstick cooking spray or lightly wipe with cooking oil, making sure it gets into any mold crevices.

4 Add half the plain gelatin to the mold. Refrigerate for 20 minutes or until the gelatin begins to set.

5 Arrange peach slices over barely set gelatin. Gently add the other half of the plain gelatin. Return mold to the refrigerator for 20 minutes or until the gelatin begins to set.

6 Add the creamy gelatin to the mold. Refrigerate for 4 hours to overnight or until the entire gelatin is completely set.

7 To unmold, place the mold in a pan with hot water to loosen up the gelatin. Remove pan from water and gently press and pull the gelatin edges away from the mold. Place a large plate or platter over mold and quickly invert gelatin onto plate. Gently remove mold. Slice, serve, and enjoy.

MARRANITOS
Pig Cookies

Marranitos are my husband's favorite pan dulce. I always make sure to grab one or two for him every time I visit the *panadería* (bakery). The cookies in this recipe are a smaller version of his favorite sweet bread. They are soft and chewy and sweetened with brown sugar. You can find a pig-shaped cookie cutter online or you can use your favorite shape.

PREPARATION TIME: 15 MINUTES
CHILL TIME: 3 HOURS TO OVERNIGHT
COOK TIME: 15 MINUTES
MAKES 25

2¼ cups all-purpose flour, divided

½ teaspoon baking soda

½ teaspoon salt

2½ teaspoons cinnamon powder

½ teaspoon ground ginger

½ teaspoon ground nutmeg

½ cup butter, room temperature

⅓ cup granulated sugar

¾ cup (packed) dark brown sugar

1½ tablespoons molasses

1 egg

1½ teaspoons vanilla extract

1   Combine 2 cups flour, baking soda, salt, cinnamon, ginger, and nutmeg in a medium bowl. Set aside.

2   Combine butter and sugars in a bowl of a stand mixer. Mix on medium speed until creamy, about 3 minutes, scraping down the sides of the bowl to make sure everything is mixed evenly.

3   Add molasses, egg, and vanilla. Mix for 2 minutes, scraping down the sides of the bowl.

4   Reduce mixer speed to low. Add flour mixture ½ cup at a time until all flour has been added and a dough forms. Cover and refrigerate dough 3 hours to overnight.

5   Remove dough from refrigerator. If dough is very hard, allow to sit for 10 minutes to soften.

6   Preheat oven to 350 degrees. Line two large baking sheets with parchment paper. Flour a working surface and rolling pin with remaining flour.

7   Roll out dough to ¼-inch thickness. Dip a 3-inch pig-shaped cookie cutter in flour and cut out pig shapes from dough. Arrange cutouts 3 inches apart on baking sheets.

8   Bake for 15 minutes or until cookie edges are set. Cool cookies on baking sheet for 5 minutes, then transfer to a cooling rack to cool completely.

9   Store in a tightly sealed container or bag. Cookies will stay soft and chewy for up to 3 days.

Dias Festivos
(Holidays)

TAMALES DE NOPALES Y PAPA

Cactus and Potato Tamales

From All Saints' Day on November 1 to Three Kings Day on January 6, our kitchen is buzzing with tamal-making camaraderie. I like to prepare a big batch and share them with family and friends, but most I freeze to serve when guests come over or when a craving creeps up. Cactus and potato tamales with salsa verde are always part of the fall and winter menu. Cactus and potato are not a common tamal combination, but when people give them a try, they are absolutely delighted.

SOAK TIME: 1 HOUR
PREPARATION TIME: 1 HOUR AND 15 MINUTES
COOK TIME: 2 HOURS
MAKES 24

40–48 corn husks

4 cups masa harina (corn flour)

1½ tablespoons baking powder

1 tablespoon salt

1½ cups vegetable shortening or lard

5 cups hot water

3 cups cooked cactus, sliced in strips (page 15)

4 russet potatoes (12 ounces), peeled and chopped into 2x½-inch wedges

salsa verde (page 34)

1   Soak corn husks in a large bowl with enough warm water to cover for at least 1 hour.

2   While husks soak, whisk together masa harina, baking powder, and salt in a large bowl.

3   Place shortening in a bowl of a stand mixer. Beat on medium speed for 10 minutes or until creamy. Continue to mix. Add dry ingredients to shortening ½ cup at a time, alternating with hot water. Masa should be wet and sticky.

4   Once masa is ready, drain corn husks and pat dry. Hold corn husk with pointy side toward you. Scoop ¼ cup masa mixture onto corn husk and spread with a spoon, leaving a 1-inch border on the sides. Place a spoonful of cactus strips, 1–2 pieces of potato, and a spoonful of salsa verde on the masa.

5   Fold one side of the corn husk over filling, then fold the other side, overlapping. Fold the pointed side up and turn over to keep tamal from unfolding. Repeat with remaining husks and masa.

6   Fill steamer with hot water right below the rack. Arrange tamales upright in steamer. Cover top of tamales with a layer of remaining husks and a damp towel, then cover with lid. Bring to a boil over medium heat, adding hot water as needed. Steam for 90 minutes or until, when tested, corn husks unwrap and masa separates easily from husks.

7   Remove tamales from steamer. Serve topped with more salsa verde.

ENSALADA NAVIDEÑA DE MANZANA

Christmas Apple Salad

Our Christmas spread could not be complete without a big bowl of this red and green apple salad. It's traditionally made with sour cream. I eventually switched over to Greek yogurt. The flavor is rich and sweet with lots of crunch.

PREPARATION TIME: 20 MINUTES
SERVES 10

1 (14-ounce) can sweetened condensed milk

16 ounces plain whole-milk Greek yogurt or sour cream, strained

4 ounces cream cheese, room temperature

2 teaspoons vanilla extract

1 (15-ounce) can peach slices in juice, chopped, plus ¼ cup canned peach juice

1 (20-ounce) can pineapple slices in pineapple juice, drained and chopped

2 red apples, chopped

2 green apples, chopped

1 cup chopped pecans, toasted

⅓ cup raisins

⅓ cup dried cranberries

demerara sugar for topping

1   Combine sweetened condensed milk, yogurt, cream cheese, vanilla, and peach juice in a blender. Blend about 30 seconds. Transfer mixture to a large serving bowl.

2   Add peaches, pineapple, apples, pecans, raisins, and cranberries. Fold ingredients together. Top with a sprinkle of sugar. Serve.

MOLE DE POLLO FÁCIL

Easy Chicken Mole

A plate of mole with turkey or chicken is one of the main offerings on a Día de Muertos altar. Because this special dish stimulates all the senses, it is intended to delight the souls that are remembered on that special day.

The traditional Mexican mole takes approximately thirty ingredients to prepare and many hours to cook. The sweet and spicy flavors slowly combine to create one of the most popular dishes in Mexico. Many home cooks can purchase jarred moles at the grocery store, but if you've always wanted to make mole sauce from scratch and never had the time, this is the perfect recipe to begin with. All the ingredients listed here are readily available at the grocery store. The cooking time is also significantly less than what traditional mole takes.

This mole sauce can also be served with potatoes, on eggs, on chilaquiles, and on enmoladas.

PREPARATION TIME: 30 MINUTES
COOK TIME: 2 ½ HOURS
SERVES 6–8

3 pounds bone-in chicken (2 legs and 1 large breast)

½ white onion, divided

4 garlic cloves, divided

2½ teaspoons salt, divided

4 tablespoons vegetable oil, divided

8 dried ancho or pasilla chiles, stems and seeds removed

4 dried guajillo chiles, stems and seeds removed

1 (90 gram) tablet Mexican chocolate

½ cup raw peanuts

½ cup pecan halves

½ cup raisins

1 Roma tomato, halved

1 banana, sliced

½ cup toasted sesame seeds plus more for garnish

2 tablespoons granulated sugar

1   Combine 12 cups water, chicken, ¼ onion, 2 garlic cloves, and 1½ teaspoons salt in a large pot. Bring to a boil over medium heat. Reduce heat to medium-low, cover, and simmer for 1 hour. Remove from heat and set aside.

2   Heat 2 tablespoons vegetable oil in a large pan over medium heat. Fry dried chile skins about 3 minutes each or until skins are soft. Do not burn.

3   Transfer chiles to a large bowl. Add 7½ cups of broth from the boiled chicken. Add the chocolate tablet and remaining 1 teaspoon salt.

4   Heat 1 tablespoon oil over medium heat in large frying pan previously used to fry chile skins. Add remaining ¼ onion, remaining 2 garlic cloves, peanuts, pecans, raisins, tomato halves, and banana to frying pan. Fry for 20 minutes, stirring frequently. Do not burn.

5   Transfer all fried ingredients and toasted sesame seeds to the large bowl where chile skins are soaking. Soak all ingredients for 40 minutes more or until chile skins are very soft and chocolate tablet has completely dissolved.

6   Transfer all soaked ingredients to blender. Blend until smooth.

7   Heat remaining tablespoon oil in a large saucepan over medium heat. Pour in sauce and stir in sugar. Continue stirring until sauce comes to a simmer, about 15 minutes. Turn off heat, cover, and keep warm.

8   Chop chicken into large pieces and add to sauce. Serve. Garnish with toasted sesame seeds.

TAMALES DE FRIJOLES Y QUESO

Pinto Bean and Cheese Tamales

Growing up, tamales were customarily made with a spicy filling to be served during posada season. (See page 221 for more about Posadas.) I grew up with only two savory choices: pork in red sauce or chicken in green sauce. "*Rojo o verde*?" That was it. These days I see so many masa flavors and filling combinations for all types of tastes.

My son loves tamales, and he also loves bean and cheese burritos. So I decided to combine the two and add these bean and cheese tamales to our holiday menu. The kids (and adults) will truly enjoy them.

PREPARATION TIME: 2 HOURS • COOK TIME: 2 HOURS
MAKES 24

40–48 corn husks

14 ounces Monterey Jack cheese, sliced into 2x½-inch wedges

Mexican cream or crème fraîche for serving

crumbled cotija cheese for serving

cilantro sprigs for serving

BEAN FILLING

1 tablespoon cooking oil

¼ white onion

2 garlic cloves

4 cups cooked pinto beans, drained (page 121)

MASA

4 cups masa harina (corn flour)

1½ tablespoons baking powder

1 tablespoon salt

1½ cups vegetable shortening or lard

4–5 cups hot water

1   Soak corn husks in a large bowl with enough warm water to cover for at least 1 hour.

2   While corn husks soak, make filling and masa. For filling, heat oil in a large skillet over medium heat. Add onion and garlic cloves. Sauté for 2 minutes. Remove onion and garlic from oil and discard.

3   Add beans. Decrease heat to medium-low and mash with a stirring motion until the beans are a chunky paste, about 15 minutes. Remove from heat and let cool. Mixture will thicken.

4   For masa, whisk together masa harina, baking powder, and salt in a large bowl.

5   Place shortening (or lard) in a bowl of a stand mixer. Beat on medium speed for 10 minutes or until creamy. Continue to mix. Add dry ingredients to shortening ½ cup at a time, alternating with hot water until masa resembles a wet paste. You might not use all the water.

6   When corn husks are done soaking, drain them and pat dry. Hold corn husk with pointy side toward you. Scoop ¼ cup masa mixture on corn husk and spread with a spoon, leaving a 1-inch border on the sides. Then add 2 tablespoons bean mixture and 1 piece of cheese.

7   Fold one side of the corn husk over filling, then fold the other side, overlapping. Fold the pointed side up and turn over to keep tamal from unfolding. Repeat with remaining husks and masa.

8   Fill steamer with hot water right below the rack. Arrange tamales upright in steamer. Cover top of tamales with a layer of remaining husks and a damp towel, then cover with lid. Bring to a boil over medium heat, adding water as needed. Steam for 90 minutes or until, when tested, corn husks unwrap and masa separates easily from husks.

9   Remove tamales from steamer. Serve warm. Remove and discard husk, drizzle with table cream, and top with cotija cheese. Garnish with cilantro sprigs.

PONCHE NAVIDEÑO

Christmas Punch

On December 16, nine days before Navidad, many Mexican families reenact the Holy Pilgrimage in a private home or a church. This tradition is known as *posada*. Each night leading to December 24, participants take turns offering up *el rosario* (rosary) and reenacting the procession, taking on the roles of the innkeepers and pilgrims.

The innkeepers stay inside the house while the pilgrims wait outside the door. The procession's dialogue is sung through a beautiful *villancico* (carol), the characters conversing back and forth until the innkeepers open the door and let the pilgrims in. That's when the celebration begins. Tamales, champurrado, and *ponche Navideño* are served, a piñata is broken, and *bolos* (goody bags) are distributed as a parting gift.

Christmas punch is a popular Mexican drink made with a variety of fruits and spices. Many families have their own version. I like to add hibiscus to give it a flowery taste. The aroma of this comforting drink is intoxicating. Your guests will not be able to get enough.

PREPARATION TIME: 10 MINUTES
COOK TIME: 30 MINUTES
SERVES 12

1 pound (about 24) tejocotes (Mexican hawthorn)

1 pound (about 3) apples

1 (6-ounce) piloncillo cone

1 (4-inch) cinnamon stick plus more for garnish

½ cup dried hibiscus flowers, rinsed and drained

4 whole cloves

3 star anise

1 pound natural sugar cane, chopped into ¾-inch-long pieces

9 dried prunes, pitted

1 pound (about 10) guavas, sliced in ¼-inch-long pieces

4 mandarins, sliced

1   Slice Mexican hawthorn into fourths and apples into eighths, removing cores. Transfer apples to a bowl with water to avoid oxidation. Set aside.

2   Heat 12 cups water in a 6-quart pot over medium heat. Bring to a boil. Add piloncillo cone, cinnamon stick, hibiscus, cloves, and star anise. Reduce heat to medium-low. Bring to a low simmer and stir.

3   Add Mexican Hawthorn, apples, sugar cane, and dried prunes. Simmer for 20 minutes.

4   Add guava and mandarin slices. Simmer for 5 minutes. Remove from heat.

5   Serve hot, scooping fruit into mugs and garnishing with cinnamon sticks.

ATOLE DE PINOLE

Pinole Atole

My mom always had a canister of pinole flour in the pantry. I never knew what she used it for, but my cousins and I would sneak into the pantry and challenge each other to take a spoonful and try to whistle. A mouthful of dry pinole would spray from our lips, followed by coughing and laughter. We never achieved anything remotely close to the sound of a whistle.

As I grew up, I realized that the pinole canister I frequently saw in the pantry and played games with was used to make my beloved atole drink I enjoyed during the fall and winter holidays.

Pinole is dried corn roasted and ground into a fine powder. Authentic pinole is sweetened with piloncillo and ground with cinnamon. Different commercial varieties include cinnamon, cacao, or sugar. Besides being used in hot and cold beverages and protein-rich breakfasts, it can also be used in baking. Pinole can be found at any Latin market or online.

COOK TIME: 35 MINUTES
SERVES 12

2 cups pinole

6 cups low-fat milk, divided

2 (4-inch) cinnamon sticks

I cup sugar

1   Whisk together pinole and 2 cups milk in a large bowl. Whisk until pinole dissolves.

2   Combine 6 cups water and cinnamon sticks in a 6-quart pot. Bring to a boil over medium heat. Stir in remaining 4 cups milk and reduce heat to medium-low.

3   Run pinole mixture through a strainer into the pot. Add sugar and stir continuously for 25 minutes. Mixture will thicken.

4   Ladle into serving cups and enjoy.

CHAMPURRADO
Masa-Based Chocolate Atole

Champurrado is a thick and cozy masa-based drink made with Mexican chocolate and milk. It is the best companion to a spicy tamal or *pan de muerto* (bread of the dead), a traditional Día de Muertos sweet bread. Traditional champurrado is made with water, but I like to make mine extra creamy with milk.

PREPARATION TIME: 10 MINUTES
COOK TIME: 40 MINUTES
SERVES 10

½ pound prepared unseasoned corn masa

1 (4-inch) cinnamon stick

3 ounces piloncillo cone

6 cups milk

2 (90-grams each) chocolate tablets

1   Place masa and 1 cup water in a blender. Blend until smooth. Set aside.

2   Place 1½ cups water in a large pot over medium heat. When water begins to boil, add cinnamon stick and piloncillo. Decrease to a low simmer. Stir to dissolve piloncillo.

3   When piloncillo has completely dissolved, add milk and chocolate tablets. Heat for 10 minutes, stirring constantly to dissolve chocolate.

4   Add masa mixture through a strainer. Stir continuously until mixture begins to boil and thicken, about 20 minutes. Serve hot.

TAMALES DE ZARZAMORA CON QUESO CREMA Y CREMA DE CHOCOLATE

Blackberry Tamales with Cream Cheese and Chocolate Cream

A big steaming pot of tamales is not complete without its own *dulce* (sweet) section. Sweet tamales are a popular dessert during the holidays, especially during the nine days of posada (page 221 for more about posadas). Served alongside a savory tamal and a comforting cup of champurrado (page 225), sweet tamales can be flavored with any fruit or spice. Some are topped with sweet cream, nuts, and even ice cream.

These blackberry tamales include a salty-sweet creamy filling wrapped around sweet masa and topped with a chocolate crema. I just love the flavors of berries and chocolate. This is my way of including one of my favorite flavor combinations into my holiday festivities.

Note: Please keep in mind that sweetness is different for everyone. Please test masa and filling sweetness to your liking before assembling and steaming.

◇◇

SOAK TIME: 1 HOUR • PREPARATION TIME: 1 HOUR 10 MINUTES
COOK TIME: 1 HOUR 40 MINUTES • MAKES 16–18

60 corn husks
12 ounces cream cheese

BLACKBERRY FILLING

3 tablespoons butter

4 cups blackberries, rinsed

½ cup granulated sugar

¼ cup dark rum

MASA

4 cups masa harina (corn flour)

1½ cups vegetable shortening, melted and slightly cooled

½ teaspoon baking powder

1½ cups granulated sugar

1 teaspoon vanilla

CHOCOLATE CREMA

1 cup Mexican cream or crème fraîche

¼ cup confectioners' sugar

¼ cup unsweetened cacao powder

1   Soak corn husks in a large bowl with enough warm water to cover for at least 1 hour.

2   Slice cream cheese into 16–18 strips.

3   To make blackberry filling, melt butter in a sauté pan over medium heat. Add blackberries and ½ cup sugar. When sugar melts, add rum. Stir frequently, gently mashing the blackberries with a wooden spoon. Cook for 10 minutes until alcohol evaporates and a chunky jam is formed.

4   To make masa filling, combine masa harina, shortening, and baking powder in a bowl of a stand mixer. Stir with spoon until mixture resembles wet sand. Add 1½ cups sugar and vanilla. Slowly add 4⅔ cups warm water until mixture resembles a wet paste. You might not use the entire quantity of water. Mix with whisk attachment for 10 minutes. Masa will be fluffy and easy to spread.

5   When corn husks are done soaking, drain them and pat dry. Hold corn husk with pointy side toward you. Scoop ⅓ cup of masa mixture on corn husk and spread with a spoon, leaving a 1-inch border on the sides. Place a cream cheese strip in the middle and top with 2 tablespoons blackberry mixture.

6   Fold one side of the corn husk over filling, then fold the other side, overlapping. Fold the pointed side up and turn over to keep tamal from unfolding. Repeat with remaining husks and masa.

7   Fill steamer with hot water right below the rack. Arrange tamales upright in steamer. Cover top of tamales with a layer of remaining husks and a damp towel, then cover with lid. Bring to a boil over medium heat, adding water as needed. Steam for 90 minutes or until, when tested, corn husks unwrap and masa separates easily from husks.

8   While tamales steam, make chocolate crema. Whisk together cream, confectioners' sugar, and cacao until well combined. (Note: Makes 1 cup.)

9   Remove tamales from steamer. Serve and top with chocolate crema.

ACKNOWLEDGMENTS

This book is a dream come true, and it could not have happened without the support of the many people in my life who have believed in me.

My husband, Efrain, who has been with me since the beginning of the journey—cheering me on, taste testing, and providing all the time and support I needed. Thank you so much for your love and constant encouragement. I love you.

Joaquin, *mijo. Te amo.* Thank you for the many hugs you gave in the kitchen. You are the best son and photography assistant anyone could ask for.

To my mom. What can I say, *Mami*? You taught me and helped shape me into what I've become. Thank you for showing that hard work pays off. You are truly the hardest-working woman I know, and I love you for it.

To my grandmother Amelia. *Mi Mamelia.* I know you are seeing this and smiling from wherever you may be. Thank you for those wonderful summers I got to spend with you and learn from you. You impacted my life greatly. I miss you. Until we meet again.

Thank you to all my *tíos, tías*, and *primos* in Mexico and California. Many meals were shared with you, and those meals have inspired me to share my story since the beginning.

Thank you, Telma, Aaron, Sophie, and Frida, for being my family and for all the infinite love and support.

Thank you to my brother-in-law Dave for accepting me into your family and for your continuous support.

Dave Zavala—thank you, *güero*, for the laughs and friendship. We truly appreciate you and see you as part of our family.

Thank you, Nicole, for sharing your ideas and listening to mine. You are the best friend and sounding board anyone could ever ask for. Thank you for all your help with the photo props I was able to include in this book. *Gracias, amiga!*

Thank you, Celeste, for your encouragement and friendship. I really appreciate all your help with taste testing and for being a great friend and neighbor.

Thank you to the Familius team. My managing editor, Brooke Jorden, and Ashlin Awerkamp, my editor, for your patience and support. Ashley Mireles, I cannot thank you enough for reaching out to me about creating this book, and thanks to Christopher Robbins for your trust and enthusiasm. I am forever grateful to all of you.

Melissa's Produce, thank you so much for the vast supplies of dried and fresh chiles. You've always been a constant supporter since the beginning of my cooking career.

Thanks to all the friends, supporters, brand managers, and PR specialists I've met through Nibbles and Feasts. You've all helped me so much in different ways throughout the years, and I could not have done this without you.

ABOUT THE AUTHOR

Ericka Sanchez is a recipe developer, food stylist, and the creator of the award-winning culinary website nibblesandfeasts.com. Ericka's cooking style is inspired by her life as a bicultural Latina living in California and her cherished memories in the kitchen with her grandmother and mother in Mexico. Ericka was born in Torreón Coahuila, Mexico, and immigrated with her family to El Paso, Texas, at eight years old.

ABOUT FAMILIUS

Visit Our Website: www.familius.com

Familius is a global trade publishing company that publishes books and other content to help families be happy. We believe that the family is the fundamental unit of society and that happy families are the foundation of a happy life. We recognize that every family looks different, and we passionately believe in helping all families find greater joy. To that end, we publish books for children and adults that invite families to live the Familius Ten Habits of Happy Family Life: love together, play together, learn together, work together, talk together, heal together, read together, eat together, give together, and laugh together. Founded in 2012, Familius is located in Sanger, California.

Connect

Facebook: www.facebook.com/familiustalk
Twitter: @familiustalk, @paterfamilius1
Pinterest: www.pinterest.com/familius
Instagram: @familiustalk

FAMILIUS

The most important work you ever do
will be within the walls of your own home.

CONVERSIONS

VOLUME MEASUREMENTS

U.S.	METRIC
1 teaspoon	5 ml
1 tablespoon	15 ml
1/4 cup	60 ml
1/3 cup	75 ml
1/2 cup	125 ml
2/3 cup	150 ml
3/4 cup	175 ml
1 cup	250 ml

WEIGHT MEASUREMENTS

U.S.	METRIC
1/2 ounce	15 g
1 ounce	30 g
3 ounces	90g
4 ounces	115 g
8 ounces	225 g
12 ounces	350 g
1 pound	450 g
2 1/4 pounds	1 kg

TEMPERATURE CONVERSION

FAHRENHEIT	CELSIUS
250	120
300	150
325	160
350	180
375	190
400	200
425	220
450	230